THE LONG WAY HOME

A Journey from South Boston to Redemption

To Patty.
My Sister in Christ.

With Love,
Bo

by

Bo McIntyre

For further information, please visit the author's website:
www.bomcintyre.com

Cover design by John Pepe
Photos by Pat Hale

First published by Dog Ear Publishing
4010 W. 86th Street, Ste H
Indianapolis, IN 46268
www.dogearpublishing.net

ISBN: 978-1-4575-2632-9

This book is printed on acid-free paper.

Printed in the United States of America

DEDICATION

This book is dedicated to:

my Mom,

(my only regret is that I didn't finish it in time);

my Uncle George, who was a real man,

and Mitchell Dyer, who instilled in me a love of books,

poetry, and crossword puzzles.

PREFACE

*M*emory is so subjective. With this in mind, I ask forgiveness from anyone who remembers differently any of the events chronicled in this book. I had two rules when I began this work: to be truthful and to relate only those occurrences of which I was part, or that I witnessed firsthand. I think that I succeeded in eliminating rumors, apocryphal antidotes and urban legends.

I have been brutally honest when writing about myself, but I have left out the names of certain others if I thought they would be unduly embarrassed by the story. My biggest dilemma was to try and spare the families of those who had their lives taken away so early without leaving out important segments of my life. If I hurt anyone I am truly sorry, that was not my intent.

The writing of this book has been both painful and cathartic. I have dredged up memories that have been suppressed, or at least kept at bay, for many years. They have triggered emotions ranging from shame to grief and there were large gaps of time when I couldn't write because I knew what had to be written next and I didn't want to remember.

I have tried to be honest and unbiased towards South Boston but even with all its faults and foibles there is something seductive that draws you to it and makes you want to stand by it as you would a friend or relative.

I'm sure I'll take some flak for being too soft on Whitey Bulger, but I tried to relate each event as I remember it, in relation to the time it occurred. I saw him do some nice things and, on one instance, was the recipient of a very generous act. On the whole, I don't think I did Whitey any favors in my portrayal of him.

To those Christians who are reading this book, I'm afraid you will have to wade through the first nine chapters before God appears in all His glory. I pushed Him out of my life very early and didn't invite Him back until very late.

In short, if this book has any redeeming message, that message is not to squander the few short years we have on this planet "chasing after the wind".

TABLE OF CONTENTS

Pages

CHAPTER 1

SOUTH BOSTON

S outhie was much more than a mere dot on a map; it was a state of mind.[1] It was a town that endowed one with a certain uniqueness, a chance to be different and yet belong to something bigger than oneself. For many a random act of birth granted them their promised fifteen minutes of fame, and for some those few minutes were enough to last a lifetime. If you were to ask the men and women of my generation and perhaps the two or three generations that followed to define themselves, the answer from far too many would be that they "came from Southie." It was as if the town was a living thing and was to be accorded one's loyalty and support as would a family member or friend. I still get upset when I hear or read of an unfair criticism of South Boston, and I haven't lived there for nearly fifty years. Its reputation today is defined by the mandated school busing years, a growing number of authors' and movie makers' concepts of the town, and the exploits of James "Whitey" Bulger, but these are merely sound bites taken out of context from a much more complex composition.

[1] Reference *The Education of Henry Adams*, page ix.

1

My story begins in the early 1950s, a more innocent time, a time before busing and the war in Viet Nam. It was a time of friendships, loyalty to those friendships, and an inherent adherence to an unspoken code, a code that we devised, believed in, and lived by. The South Boston I knew wasn't a united community but a geographical area consisting of multiple neighborhoods, and from a kid's viewpoint, a neighborhood was defined by the corner he hung out on. In fact, when we referred to South Boston, we really meant our small section of the town. There were major sectional divisions, such as City Point, the Lower End, the D street, the Old Colony, and the Mary Ellen McCormack (Old Harbor) housing projects, and within these distinct sections there were numerous corner gangs, which were all entities unto themselves. I should add that the great majority of the gangs were simply a group of kids who came together for friendship, sports, and in order to belong. There were only two or three groups that would fit today's definition of a street gang. Until forced busing of the 1970s united the town under a common cause, there was no homogeneous place called South Boston; it didn't exist.

The neighborhood I knew and lived in was at the corner of O and 2nd Streets, and it stretched from 1st Street to 3rd Street east to west and P Street to N Street north to south. This was the extent of our world, and within that tiny piece of the city, we were virtually self-sufficient. We had a Metropolitan Transit Authority (the MTA, made famous by the Kingston Trio's song about Charlie) bus terminal, which was about a twenty-minute ride to downtown Boston, a spa that served breakfast, lunch, and dinner, a sandwich shop that served submarine sandwiches (we called them "spuckies"), a tailor/dry cleaner, a convenience store, a mini supermarket with a delicatessen counter, a barroom, and a butcher shop. The adjoining block offered a barbershop, two drugstores, and a second convenience store. There was a Catholic church, a parochial elementary school, and a girls' parochial high school. We were bordered on the north by docks that were main venues for unloading cargo ships and ports for United States Naval vessels, on the east and south by the seashore and its beaches, and on the west by a great sports field complex and a grassy, tree-studded park with a view of the waterfront and the Boston skyline.

Within walking distance or a five-minute bus ride was the East Broadway shopping district that included a major clothing store, two supermarkets, a fish market, a butcher shop, a movie theater (one of two in the town), a hardware store, a bicycle repair shop, a pool room/bowling alley, a package store, a couple of bar-rooms, a drugstore, a public library, and Slocum's, a toy store that offered just about any toy, model building kit for cars, planes, trains, or anything else you could imagine. The shop was long and narrow with every available space crammed full of wonderful, unexpected treasures that would keep a kid shopping for hours trying to find that one great toy to fit his budget, which usually didn't exceed twenty-five cents. Further on East Broadway, on a hill that separated East Broadway from West Broadway, was the location of a number of doctors', dentists' and lawyers' offices. The natives referred to it as "Pill Hill" because of the number of doctors located there. The hill also con-tained the South Boston Municipal Court and, in the same building as the courthouse, a gym with handball and basketball courts and public showers. A few doors away were a large candlepin bowling alley and a coffee shop. It was no wonder there were so few car owners in the neigh-borhood or that very few women had driver's licenses; there was little need for either.

The majority of the families were lower-middle-class, blue-collar workers whose husbands worked while the wives were, in most circumstances, mothers and homemakers. The dwellings were from two-to six-family tenement buildings with an occasional one- family home and a row of five or six townhouses.

Privacy was virtually nonexistent. Everyone knew their neighbors well and, because of the proximity of the living quarters, perhaps too well. For the most part everyone was aware of their neighbor's circumstances, and there were very few matters that remained hidden, especially from those who lived in the same tenement. This lack of privacy had its pros and cons. We all had things we'd rather not have shared with the world, and the simple realization that it would be revealed sometimes had a constraining influence before the fact. I'm convinced if there was only one benefit this physical closeness provided, it was a relational closeness. We all knew we were neither less flawed nor any more perfect than our neighbors, and this awareness fostered a feeling of empathy and an understanding of each other's trials and tribulations. This is not to say we lived in some social utopia where everyone loved and cared for one another without a suggestion of strife; we didn't. If the immediacy of our living conditions created a personal bonding, then it, by necessity, produced a certain tension. The people of South Boston have two admirable traits: they have a fierce sense of loyalty to friends and family and to the town, and they "tell it as it is" (I personally detest this phrase, but it defines the South Boston mind-set perfectly). There is never a doubt where one stands with Southie folks; they are honest to a fault. Although this attitude could and did lead to verbal confrontations, short-term quarrels, and even an occasional fistfight, it was usually just that—short term. These sorts of encounters helped to clear the air and, more times than not, ended with an apology and a handshake.

I've noticed the pundits of the print media like to use the word "insular" when they wish to criticize South Boston or any of the other ethnic neighborhoods in Boston. A more apt phrase would be "taking care of one's own." The people in the neighborhood watched out for each other: they helped to pay rents and buy groceries for a family who may be experiencing financial difficulties, they provided dinners to ailing neighbors, they helped to clean houses and babysit when there was a new birth in a family. If an argument between a husband and wife got out of hand and threatened to become physical, the neighbors would talk the husband out of the house, sometimes overnight if alcohol was involved. I recall one incident when a peeping Tom was thought to be stalking a local girl. For three nights the men in the neighborhood staked out the girl's home, and when, on the fourth night, the offender showed up (he turned out to be a local guy), he was slapped around, and the embarrassment of being caught drove him to move from the area. The neighborhood policed itself and was virtually crime-free. In all my years there, the only time the police were called to the area was to chase the kids off the corner because of excessive noise or for playing ball in the street. There was never a break-in, a stolen car, an armed robbery, a purse-snatching, or anything of that ilk, not one. We never locked our doors until it was time to go to bed. The media, in later years, dismissed the low crime rate by insisting it was so low in South Boston because the crimes went unreported due to the town's "code of silence." This was simply not true.

Crimes against society were another matter. Most people played the street number every day. There were

THE LONG WAY HOME

numerous "bookies" who would take your bet, including my father at various times in his life. The local barroom, the neighborhood store, and even the MTA bus terminal had a guy who would handle your action. There was even one bookie that went door to door. You could wager as little as a nickel, and if you picked three numbers in the correct order, you would get back thirty dollars. A dollar bet would get you six hundred dollars (as much as two months' wages back then). The operation worked something like this: they would add the handle (the amount bet at Suffolk Downs, the local horse-racing track) on the first race's win, place, and show bets and divide by the number of bets. For instance, if the amount bet on the first race was $10,480 and the number of bettors was 200, the resulting number would be $502.40 ($10,480 divided by 200). If you repeat the process for the handle of the third race and then the fifth race, the result might look like this:

1st race	$ 502.40
3rd race	$ 480.60
5th race	$ 618.20

The daily number was ascertained by reading down, from top to bottom, the numbers just to the left of the decimal point. In this example the daily number would be 208, and if you played a fourth number (the payoff for four numbers was about $5,000), that number was the first digit to the right of the decimal point for the 5th race. In this case the number would have been 2082. Three-and four-number plays were the most common bets, but there were a number of exotic wagers. You could bet the number would come out in exact order, which was the highest payoff; or any order for three-and four-number combinations, which paid less; or you could bet on single digits, which would pay about 8 to 1. The odds of picking three numbers in the exact order was about 1,000 to 1, but the bookies would pay 600 to 1 on a hit; the difference was the "vigorish" or the "vig," their profit margin.

Now, this grouping of numbers is entirely meaningless and could not have served any other purpose except as a gambling tool. The newspaper industry was knowingly complicit in this illegal activity by printing this set of numbers in their evening edition, which hit the streets about 7 p.m. and was snatched up as quickly as it hit the newsstands by thousands of buyers who bought it for the sole reason of determining the nightly number. The newspapers stopped printing the street number after Massachusetts got into the numbers game, and they now print the Massachusetts State Lottery number solely, virtually destroying the illegal numbers racket. They could have put the bookies out of business fifty years ago by ceasing to print the handles. I've always been curious to learn how and by whom the original deal was struck between organized crime and the major newspapers of the time.

Another illegal activity that was accepted, condoned, and anticipated by the community was the purchase of stolen or "hot" goods. There were a number of men in the neighborhood who worked the docks as longshoremen, and once in a while a shipping container would "accidentally" slip its cables and break open in the hold of a ship. In the cleanup some of the goods would be "gone missing" until they reappeared in the neighborhood, usually in the trunk of a car. Most of the contraband was foodstuffs such as cans of tuna fish or crabmeat but sometimes clothing items like sneakers, sweaters, and jackets would become available, and as soon as the word was out, there was a mad dash to sort through the apparel to get the right size before it was sold out. In later years another source of these goods was hijacked trucks or trucks making deliveries to the retail stores in the area. We, the neighborhood kids, were usually responsible when goods disappeared from the delivery trucks.

Not everyone in the neighborhood played the numbers or participated in the purchase of "hot" merchandise, and the ones who didn't probably condemned those activities as wrong. But for the people who did play the numbers and did buy stolen goods, the majority didn't act out of greed. The street number represented a daily chance for a windfall that could make things a little better financially for the winner by catching up on their electric bill or paying the corner store owner the money they owed from getting milk and bread "on the cuff" (credit). Sure the odds were against hitting the number, but it offered hope and gave them something to look forward to six days a week, and isn't hope what keeps us all going? As for buying stolen goods, for most it was the only chance many had to provide new sneakers or a sweater or a winter coat for their children at a price they could afford.

I don't wish to be an apologist for their actions, but neither am I going to judge them. There were times in my life when I would have done just about anything to provide the things my family needed. I should add the neighborhood drew the line on what "hot" goods they would or would not buy. They wouldn't buy anything they suspected of being stolen from an individual, or from a house or a car, or even from a small business such as a corner store. They were under the misconception it was okay to buy goods stolen from corporations, delivery trucks, anything from the docks, and to rip off insurance companies by any scam possible. They regarded it as a kind of class struggle, and by taking a little back, they felt they were exacting a kind of revenge on the big shots who ran things and controlled their lives through their riches and their ownership of the country. Back then I wholeheartedly agreed with and participated in the process by buying, stealing, and selling stolen goods. Today I simply understand it.

The typical family in my neighborhood (if there is any such thing as a typical family, or a typical anything for that matter) consisted of a father, mother, and two to four kids. The father was, usually, the breadwinner, while the mother maintained the home and raised the kids. I can't recall one mother in my neighborhood who worked outside of the home. There was very little contact with the man of the family. He would come home from work and, after eating his supper, listen to the radio or watch television until it was time for bed. The infrequent communication between the father and his kids took place if he was needed to apply discipline for some infraction reported to him by his wife. This didn't happen very often, since most of the mothers felt their job was to keep peace, or at least an uneasy truce, between the "old man" (another expression I hated and never used) and his kids. A catchphrase that I heard over and over, not only in my house but in the houses of my friends, was "Don't tell your father or there'll be hell to pay." It seemed as if there was one big conspiracy by the mother of the household to keep the father uninformed about what was occurring in his own home. In retrospect, however, I realize he, the father, was complicit in the course of action, and that the husband and the wife had a tacit agreement to exclude him from all but the most important of transgressions. He all but assured this process would continue by overreacting every time he was called on to provide some guidance, advice, or leadership by making the situation so uncomfortable and upsetting to the entire family with his ranting and raving that it was much less traumatic to simply keep the truth from him. Ostensibly the father was the head of the family, but in reality the mother controlled the everyday functions of the home and the raising of the kids.

The most far-reaching influence provided by the father was to model how a *man* was supposed to act. Most of the male role models in my life seemed as if they were cloned. They espoused the same values, lived their lives in the same manner, and taught their kids the same lessons. A man had to be willing to physically defend himself and never, ever show any physical or emotional weakness. On the surface these may be words to live by, but they assume everyone is of the same temperament, and they set up kids of a more sensitive nature to fail. Some of the toughest people I know and the people I admire most are those who never had a fistfight in their lives, but stand up for their beliefs no matter the consequences. I went from a sensitive, innocent kid who avoided confrontations at all costs to a violence-addicted teenager who went looking for a fight wherever I might find one. And the reason I reversed my behavior was because I was so tired of going against the tide, and I lacked the inner strength, the genuine fortitude to weather the storm and live as my conscience dictated and not sell out to the world because the going got tough. I met only two men in my life who accepted me as I was and, more importantly, liked me that way. One was my mother's brother, my uncle, George Young, and the other was a friend of the family, Mitchell Dyer, whom I loved dearly. Coincidentally, neither of whom came from South Boston.

The point I'm trying to make is that fighting was not only accepted but expected by everyone—and I mean everyone from our parents to the police. This attitude fostered a fatal flaw for many. There was a thread of violence woven through the fabric of the community, creating a culture of conflict. The danger was that some of us never grew out of reverting to confrontation as a method for settling disputes, and its acceptance allowed the violence to escalate to its ultimate conclusion.

Some of the things I miss most about our neighborhood are the little things that were taken for granted but have long since disappeared. One is the cordiality everyone had for one another. When we passed someone walking down the street, we not only smiled and said hello, but we actually looked them in the eyes. Try that now and watch the reaction of the other person: they'll either turn their head away or look at you as if you were crazy or dangerous or both. We swore like troopers but never in front of a female or a young kid, and if you slipped your peers would warn you to "watch your language." I swore so badly that I often inserted the "F" bomb between letters in a word, such as "un-F—-ing-believable." We always helped the ladies in the neighborhood with their bags of groceries by carrying them to their flats. A friend of mine, Tom King, was always nice to my mother, whether carrying her bags from the bus stop to our house or simply in general conversation, and my mother thought the world of him. She once told me she wished I would hang around with Tom more because he was such a gentleman. Tom King was one of the most dangerous guys in the town, a stone-cold killer. Being nice can take you a long way.

I miss the hot summer nights when all the neighbors would spend most of the night sitting on their steps trying to catch a breath of cool air that might sporadically waft down 2nd Street from the ocean while us kids would play our various street games or simply revel in the adults' conversations, because we could learn more about our parents when they were relating stories to the neighbors than when we were together at home. I miss neighbors like Mrs. Paulanthony, whose house was next door to us and who would tap on our window across the alley separating our houses with a broomstick to invite my mother over to her house to take a bath because she knew we didn't have a bathtub. We had an army-surplus rubber bathtub that we unfolded in the kitchen, heated the water on the stove, and after bathing, bailed the water from the tub, folded it up, and stored it in a closet. After the exertion of emptying the tub of water and putting it away, we needed another bath. And, on another night, across that same alley, she shouted out directions on how to administer a bath of alcohol to bring my baby sister out of a seizure brought on by a high fever.

I fondly recall those long summer days spent in M Street Park, playing baseball from eight o'clock in the morning until dusk and then sitting under the street lamp on 2nd Street playing whist until all hours of the morning. Those were the days and nights of innocence before we realized we were poor, before we thought this endless summer called adolescence might ever have an end, and before the real world elbowed its way into our lives, changing everything forever and not always for the best.

I was always struck by the confidence and utter lack of fear that South Boston kids possessed. They weren't afraid of anything, and it was more than just the misplaced idea of youth that they were bullet proof. They were aware bad things could happen but were willing to take a chance, to push the envelope, and damn the consequences. Some would call it foolhardy, some courage or even cockiness, but whatever label you wish to attach, it was an attitude that South Boston kids carried with them into every endeavor they attempted, whether it was fighting in foreign wars, fighting fires, serving on the police force, street fighting, in the sports arena, business, politics, or even criminal activity.

If war is the ultimate test of a man's courage, then the men of South Boston have earned an A-plus. Their record is both extraordinary and tragic. James Webb, a former Secretary of the Navy, Marine Corps hero, and author, has stated on radio talk shows that if the rest of the nation had suffered losses at the same ratio as South Boston, the number of servicemen killed in action would have more than doubled. Since the Spanish-American War, South Boston has had a greater ratio of volunteers and the highest wartime casualty rate per capita of any community in the country. There are approximately 150 squares in South Boston named after men killed in action in the various wars since WWI with 19 killed in Korea and 25 in Viet Nam alone. I find these numbers astonishing for a town with a population of about thirty thousand.

Pat Loftus has stated in his excellent book *That Old Gang of Mine: A History of South Boston* (from which I borrowed the statistics noted in the preceding paragraph) his belief that for the kids of South Boston, "...the battle field was merely an extension of the football field." I'm of the opinion the very values that governed their actions in times of extreme stress were instilled in them long before they were introduced to football. These strong feelings of duty, pride, courage, and, above all, loyalty were inherited from hundreds if not thousands of generations of their European ancestors. When the first of these ancestors immigrated here, instead of being amalgamated into America's "melting pot," they sought each other out and created neighborhoods that most resembled their way of life as it was in the "old country," allowing them to retain and even nurture their spiritual and moral beliefs. The areas claimed by the various ethnic groups became enclaves where the earth- shattering event of pulling up stakes and moving to another continent, in effect to another world, was tempered by being welcomed into a community that spoke the same language, practiced the same religion, and held the same social mores.

In the 1950s Boston had a number of these ethnic strongholds left over from the 19th century. East Boston and the North End were predominately Italian, the South End and parts of Roxbury and Dorchester were African American, while South Boston and Charlestown were, for the most part, Irish. After WWII the displaced persons from Eastern Europe who fled Communism from places like Lithuania and Poland carved out small areas of the existing neighborhoods. Instead of slowly integrating over the years, these ethnic areas became more singular, and the hostility between the groups was always bubbling just below the surface. Although the original contention between them was economic, with the various groups vying for the same jobs, by the 1950s it had deteriorated into pure racism and ethnic bias.

This self-imposed isolation from the rest of the city fostered South Boston's feeling of being special and reinforced its belief that its embrace of duty, pride, courage, and loyalty were what separated South Boston from the rest of the world. These values were learned at a very early age, and they were learned not by teaching, but by trial and error. A child soon learned what behavior was accepted and those behaviors that would not be tolerated. Duty, pride, courage, and loyalty were not just nice-sounding words to be tossed around haphazardly; they were words to live by and, for some, to die by.

This combination of fearlessness and the acceptance of violence as a means of settling disputes proved, for many, to be a deadly mixture.

CHAPTER 2

FAITH INTERRUPTED

*G*od was with me. As far back as I can remember, I
felt the presence of Him in my life. I knew He had
a plan for me and that He was guiding and protecting me.
I had little or no religious teaching; consequently I didn't
know who God was nor did I know anything about Christ,
who I thought was simply the human son of God. The
only thing I knew about the Holy Spirit was when I heard
my Catholic neighbors mention the Holy Trinity and the
Holy Ghost. I prayed the Lord's Prayer every night and
asked God to bless a handful of people, most of whom
were deceased and likely beyond prayer. Everything I
knew or, rather sensed—about God was instinctual, yet it
was more real than anything I had ever experienced. I
knew God was good and I wanted to please Him, and
whatever the consequences, I was determined to do the
right thing. I don't know what came first, trying to please
God or my highly active conscience, a conscience that has
plagued me for my entire life. My first nine or ten years
were lived in uncompromising honesty and basking in the
light of God's pleasure. I knew He loved me and blessed
me. I was a straight "A" student, excelled on the sports

field, and, although I preferred to be solitary, I was continually thrust into positions of leadership. I was aware, even then, these attributes were a gift from God.

The world had other plans. Being good doesn't win many friends, and being your own confidante can make for a lonely occupation. My righteousness didn't stem from a need to impress others with my virtue, nor did I want to do the right thing because I was taken in by some parental propaganda designed to make their jobs easier, but because I believed with all my heart and soul we were supposed to be moral and upright and, for want of a better word, good. There's a price to be paid for this behavior, however, and I paid dearly. During my adolescent years, my conscience reigned supreme. Even now, I wonder how one so young could have had such a grasp on what was right and what was wrong. Only God was capable of conveying such knowledge. My every action was ruled by my conscience and, counter to the mantra of an approaching era, if it wasn't "good," I didn't do it. I walked a straight and narrow path, so narrow there was barely room enough for me. Although it may be easy for people to admire goodness in others, it's almost impossible for them to want to be associated with a "saint" for very long. Although I never foisted my morals on those around me, I never failed to "march to my own drummer." Who wants to be friends with someone who, by his behavior, continually reminds one of his own too human foibles? The consequences of my actions and refusal to compromise led to a solitary existence and a constant emotional battering.

I hated school. The incessant anxiety and dread I felt in any social setting were multiplied tenfold in a schoolroom environment. There were many nights I lay awake worrying about an impending talk I may have had to deliver or a question I may be called on to answer. I agonized over not having the correct response because that would represent failure, and failure would be devastating to my self-worth. The worst-case scenario would have been to be laughed at, and, because of the fragility of my ego, to become a laughingstock would have destroyed me completely. I knew I must not fail. Therefore, every correct answer, each perfect grade increased a self-imposed pressure to succeed, or not to fail, and increased the expectations imposed on me by others. This was a formula for disaster. School was a battleground on which I was continually attacked on two fronts. I was determined to be good both behaviorally and scholastically, and, if the pressure wasn't tough enough, my compulsion to be perfect led to a second and much more difficult challenge. Kids aren't exactly enamored with their classmates who are considered smart and well behaved. The good kids achieve the reputation of "teacher's pet," usually well deserved; because the teacher, as those in any walk of life, will turn to the person whom he or she can expect to perform in a predictable and responsible manner. My behavior didn't help me win friends and influence people. As each school year progressed, the teasing became more vicious and more hurtful, and there were times I was so beaten down I wanted to intentionally fail a test or give the teacher a hard time just to endear me to my classmates and end the emotional pain. I wanted to be accepted and to be one of the guys, but I wasn't yet ready to turn my back on a God whose love was the only thing that sustained me.

I despised confrontations so I rarely reacted to the taunts of the other kids unless the words deteriorated to a challenge of my manhood. Any time words such as coward, sissy, yellow, etc. were hurled at me, I would lose all self-control, and I would go after my tormentor with both fists flying. For days after such an incident, the insults of my classmates would cease, replaced by stony silence and avoidance, which was like heaven to me. All I really wanted was to be left alone. The problem was whether I won or lost the fight, I became guilt-ridden as my conscience reared its ugly head and drove me into a mood bordering on depression. In retrospect, there wasn't any way I could sustain my beliefs for a lifetime, because I simply didn't have the foundation on which to build the permanent life-style of a God follower. My faith was built on sand, not on solid ground, and wanting to please God and to be accepted by those who populated my world was becoming increasingly impossible to reconcile. I wasn't strong enough to battle these demons alone, and there wasn't anyone in my life who was capable of teaching me the ways of God. I turned to the Bible, but the wording of whatever version I had available seemed to be written in a foreign language, and I was left as ignorant as ever.

I held on for a while longer. The few friends I made had a couple of things in common: they were kids who wanted to get good grades, behave in class, and just get along, and we experienced like instances of harassment and bullying in retaliation for our behavior. I attended the Bigelow school in South Boston from midway in the third grade through the sixth and hung around almost exclusively with three kids. They were Bobby Cummings, Paulie Wieners, and Roger LeClair, two of whom met tragic endings.

Bobby and I were friends, but there was an unspoken competition between us centered on who was the best student and who received the highest grades. Since we were both straight "A" students, a clear winner never emerged. We were so far ahead of the rest of the class that our fifth grade teacher, Mr. Bostwick, removed us from the class-room, set up a couple of tables in the cloakroom, and allowed us to research potential professions and work on special projects for the entire school year, only visiting the classroom to take the required quizzes and examinations.

There was a local radio program called "Quiz Down" hosted by Nelson Bragg, a well-known emcee and DJ on station WCOP, that arranged competitions between the Boston elementary schools based on general knowledge. Bobby and I were chosen, along with three other kids, to participate against the Gavin, another South Boston school. The events of that night haunt me even today. I had the correct answer for all three questions posed to me, while Bobby missed the two asked of him. The program was held in our school's auditorium, and, as we were in the cloakroom putting on our coats preparing to go home, Bobby turned his back on me and began to stare out of the window. I noticed his shoulders were quivering, and I real-ized he was crying. My first reaction was a feeling of relief and thankfulness that God had blessed me once again and that it wasn't me staring out of the window with tear-filled eyes. What I did next caught even me by complete sur-prise. I buttoned my coat and, without even saying good night to Bobby, I went home. Even worse, I wasn't sorry he had failed, but proud of myself for finally besting him. This was the first time in my life I had acted out of pure selfishness and experienced elation at the expense of another's misery. When I recall that night, I still flush with shame. I would give anything to have walked up to Bobby and put an arm around him or at least given him an encouraging word. This was a pivotal event in my walk with God. I didn't know anything about repentance and forgiveness; I wasn't aware that Christ died to redeem this very sin, and I was forgiven even before I committed it.

My concept of following God when tempted to sin was that I must grit my teeth, clench my fists, and, through sheer willpower, walk away from the sinfulness of the act. I believed each failure to do so was noted by God and was an ineradicable mark, a sort of scorecard of bad behavior that accumulated until it reached some finite number that would finally exhaust God's patience and expel me from His presence. The events of that night planted a seed of unworthiness in my psyche, and it began to take root and sprout as weeds in a garden. I only knew I had failed to do the right thing, and I sensed I wouldn't survive too many more such failures without surrendering this struggle, which was becoming increasingly more difficult to sustain.

Bobby, unlike me, remained disciplined and lived up to his potential. He went on to college and a good profession. Tragically, years later in July 1973, he was killed in a plane crash at Logan Airport, returning from a business trip. Ironically, his father, who was an officer with the Massachusetts State Police, was stationed at Logan and was in charge of the rescue operations on the day of the accident.

Roger LeClair, Paulie Wieners, and I spent a lot of afternoons after school at M Street Park playing the usual sports: baseball in the spring and football in the fall. Roger was a quiet kid who tended to stay in the background (a trait most "good" kids had in common) to avoid calling attention to himself, which only invited the harassment that was sure to follow. He was a big kid, overweight but physically strong, with an endearing personality and a great heart. One day the three of us were playing a variation of tackle football, and I noticed whenever I was carrying the ball or blocking for Paulie, Roger was easily knocked down or run over. I silently congratulated myself on my newfound athletic prowess until a few days later, when we heard Roger had contracted polio. On the following day, as we entered our classroom, we were shocked to see an empty space where Roger's desk had once stood. It had been removed to prevent the spread of the virus, and the whole classroom reeked of disinfectant. A few days later we were told by our teacher that Roger had died. There wasn't any trauma counseling in those days, and no adult even thought to ask who may have been exposed to the disease through contact with Roger. We went on as if nothing out of the ordinary had occurred. His name was never mentioned in that classroom again, but we were reminded of Roger every day by the empty space where his desk had once stood and the lingering odor of disinfectant. I remember thinking not only how fragile life is but how soon a lost life is forgotten, relegated to some recess in one's mind, and the memory of that life is recalled only when it suits one's motives. Roger was the first friend of mine to die young, but he was only the first of too many.

My father didn't like me very much. Except for looking alike and a couple of similar personality traits, we had little in common. I took after my mother's side of the family, and my father began to resent me for reasons that are hard to explain, except that we thought so differently. He was a man who settled his differences with his fists; whenever possible I avoided confrontations. He once told me he had read only one book in his life; I was an avid reader. He was a "Jack of all trades" who could do anything with his hands—carpentry, electrical work, or plumbing; I hated anything to do with these activities and avoided them at all costs. Some of my worst days were trying to help my father build or repair something; invariably I was told to leave because I was "useless." I loved sports and music; he didn't understand the attraction of either, especially music. I was good in school; he got as far as the fourth grade. I don't think it possible for a father and son to be more dissimilar.

When I was very young, I did everything in my power to try and please him, but he found it very difficult to offer praise or to show affection. My father never once hit me, but his words cut like a knife, and I soon learned to tune him out. He wasn't an ogre nor was he unique; he was one of a whole generation of fathers who kept their thoughts and their feelings to themselves. I understand where he was coming from; I would spend some time there myself. I bring up my relationship with my father not to lay blame, but to explain. Look, we are all the sum of our experiences, and one's father has great influence on one's emotional and spiritual growth, especially in those formative years of adolescence. My father was but one influence of many that contributed to the person I became. It wouldn't be too far in the future when he would be added to the rapidly growing list of those whom I wouldn't allow to have any impact on my life. I would soon encounter one of those forks in the road that we all confront at one time or another, and the road I chose would determine the path I'd follow for years to come.

My world was becoming a very hurtful place, and I was becoming an emotional coward. God's presence was growing distant and would soon disappear completely. I was sure He had written me off as unworthy. I became overly sensitive and plagued by a social anxiety so over-powering, at times, it could and did incapacitate me. I was physically fearless but words wounded me to the quick, and any form of rejection induced in me a feeling of inad-equacy so overwhelming I was literally unable to speak for hours at a time. I felt safe only when I was in the company of my most faithful friends—my books. They lifted me from the crowded tenements and the angry voices and the conflicts of the city. They introduced me to heroic characters who accepted me into their world without reservation and who never disappointed. I was transported to exotic places like Treasure Island and Sherwood Forest; I sailed aboard the *Bounty* and the *Pequod* and battled Napoleon's Navy as a shipmate of Lt. Hornblower. I solved baffling mysteries with the Hardys and Sherlock Holmes and roamed the streets of London alongside Oliver and Mr. Hyde. I would rush home from school to our cold-water flat, light the oven, and sit in front of the stove with my feet propped on the open oven door for warmth, reading *The Last of the Mohicans* or *From the Earth to the Moon* until suppertime. Then, after hurrying through my meal, I would crawl into bed and read until it was impossible to keep my eyes open any longer. The only conflict my books presented was returning them to the library. I hated to give them back and held onto them until the last possible moment because handing them over to the librarian was akin to saying goodbye to someone I loved and whom I may never meet again.

Darkened moving-picture theaters were another refuge where, for three hours, I would lose myself in a story being played out by larger-than-life actors on larger-than-life screens. The classic novels and the movies of the 1950s reinforced the belief that right always bests wrong, the good guy always wins, and that God exists. I was still clinging to the hope God would take me back, and I needed to believe right and wrong weren't merely subjective assumptions. I desperately had to embrace these concepts as truths, because I knew I was in danger of slipping away.

I was tired of fighting the battle. It seemed the more I tried to do the right thing, the more I suffered for the effort. I remembered reading somewhere that "no good act goes unpunished," and I began to experience it firsthand. The reward for my moral behavior was to become a social pariah, to get emotionally beaten up by classmates and even by family. My father didn't think I was tough enough, and my aunts referred to me as an "odd duck." Their words wounded me so deeply and hurt so badly that I had to end the pain somehow. My self-confidence was eroded almost daily, and there was no one I could turn to for solace. I have always been hard on myself and avoided self-pity or transferring blame to others for any misfortunes that may have befallen me. However, allow me this one show of regret. When I think back to the years when I was five to nine or ten years old, I don't relive them; I observe them. I see a boy who is struggling to accomplish nothing more than to follow God, to act how we are supposed to act, to love and be loved and to be accepted, and I watch him fail. It breaks my heart and I long to reach out, put my arms around him, and tell him it will be all right, but I can't and it wasn't. God was nowhere to be found, and I didn't know where to look.

The solution came to me suddenly and dramatically and led to one of those life-changing choices that we encounter every so often in this experience we call living. As odd as it seems, given its importance, I don't recall the exact words nor what precipitated them, only that my father said something hateful to me, something probably no worse than words he had hurled at me a hundred times before. What I do remember is going to my room, closing the door, and vowing out loud to "never let him or anyone else ever hurt me again." I was nine or ten years old and already weary of this wanton world. I looked deep within myself and discovered a secret, safe place. I hurried inside, closed the gate, and barred the door. Except for a few instances of weakness, I kept my heart locked away in this place, safe from the slings and arrows of this hurtful world, for most of my life. I became adept at keeping people at just the right distance: close enough to appear caring yet far enough away to protect me from being vulnerable. Whenever someone conned their way in or stormed the gate, I learned a valuable lesson and doubled the guard so as not to be fooled again. The irony is that if you won't feel, you can't love; you can't know joy or peace and, worst of all, you can't know God. Your very soul will atrophy. Soon the only feelings I was capable of were anger or sadness in the form of depression and, in my case, depression was nothing more than suppressed anger. I tried to keep my anger in check because when it exploded, it put my conscience into active mode and, as time went by, I found myself struggling more to control it and succeeding less.

I don't want to give the impression that I'm blaming my personal frailties on my parents for not loving me enough or loving me too much, or for being too strict or not strict enough, or being involved too much or not being involved enough. My parents did the best they could with what they had. They never once hurt me physically nor purposely wounded me emotionally, and I never went hungry, always had clean clothes, and knew they had my back. We very rarely hear of a parent robbing a bank or getting hooked on drugs because their kids disappointed them. Why, then, do we excuse our own inappropriate behavior because of our relationship with our parents or what our parents may or may not have done to us? I apologize to those kids who were horribly abused and who have every right to deal with that betrayal by any means they deem fitting. My point is that every parent, including you and me, is far from perfect, and we all leave some kind of emotional scar on our kids. We need to stop blaming, forgive, and go on with our lives. The only one we can control is ourselves.

I became a poser. Despising who I was, I recreated myself by inventing a character whose persona I shaped and molded to be the person I wished I were. I borrowed, or rather appropriated as my own, personality traits and characteristics from those I admired and from movie roles and characters from the many books I had read. I even concocted a new, distinctive way of walking that hinted at a slight swagger by the movement of my shoulders, yet giving the impression of humility by keeping my head bowed. The "good" bad guy, so popular in the movies during the fifties, was whom I admired and tried to emulate. That this character usually laid down his life, often with guns blazing, for something or someone of greater value only made him more attractive. The most essential element of this charade was that no one must ever be allowed to observe the failed, flawed individual who existed in that secret place behind the closed gate and the barred door. Even though I still suffered from an extreme case of social anxiety, I became so adept at playing this role that if I stayed in character, I could make a connection with a few selected people and actually have a relationship of some worth. The irony was they liked this other kid who didn't exist; he was an actor playing a part in some deranged drama, and there were times when even I wasn't sure which was the real me.

Boston Latin School was a prestigious exam school located in Boston between the Fenway and Huntington Avenue. The school was founded in 1635, and some of its graduates were Samuel Adams, Ralph Waldo Emerson, John Hancock, Joseph Kennedy, Cotton Mather, George Santayana, and Theodore White (Benjamin Franklin attended Latin but didn't graduate), just to name a few illustrious names, but its rolls are replete with men who made a difference. There are a number of governors, architects, and movers and shakers in academia, business, politics, and religion who obtained a formidable foundation on which to build their future education at this great institution. I was accepted to the school beginning in the seventh grade, and because of my grades, I wasn't required to take an acceptance examination. My first year went well, and my grades were good enough to get my name on the honor roll or, as the school designated it, "Approbation with Distinction."

The collapse came suddenly. I was in my second year at Boston Latin School, the eighth grade, and literally over night the pressure valve finally let go, and I simply quit trying to overachieve, stopped trying to be good, and stopped caring about my grades. I was just so tired of trying so hard. I longed to have friends and to cease being a loner. I wanted to belong to something bigger than myself; I wanted to be around people who hadn't any expectations of me and with whom I didn't have to be perfect, and not to have to experience the guilt and regret that accompanies performing below one's ability. I soon discovered that I would much rather read, watch television, or play sports than study, and my grades began to suffer. The first report card of the year produced the first "C" grades I had ever received, and when I experienced the thing I dreaded most—failure—I realized the consequences weren't as bad as I had imagined. Pandora's jar was uncorked and I realized I didn't have to be perfect; I didn't have to subjugate myself to the constant pressure and anxiety I had been living with for as long as I can remember. I was less than perfect and the world didn't end.

My grades continued to slip, not surprising since I never opened a book and I was attending one of the toughest public schools in the country. I was forced to repeat the eighth grade. Only a year ago, this event would have been such a traumatic blow, such an embarrassment and feeling of failure, that I may have literally contemplated suicide. Now it mattered little. The repercussions of failure were, surprisingly, inconsequential because I chose to fail. I felt free for the first time in my life. I passed my second try at the eighth grade and barely eked by the ninth. I transferred to South Boston High for my sophomore year. Well, at least my exit from Latin School had one positive: a common experience with Benjamin Franklin. We both failed to graduate.

This was the first time I had failed to finish something I had started, but it proved only to be the initial emergence of a trait that would cause me and the people close to me a lot of problems in the years to come. From this point on, whenever I mastered anything, I quickly lost interest and walked away.

South Boston High didn't offer much of a scholastic challenge. The curriculum was the same as the one I had been exposed to in the seventh, eighth, and ninth grades at Latin School, only a great deal less demanding, and I was able to skate by with a minimum of effort. My newfound freedom was exhilarating. I didn't have to answer to anyone, and I did what I wanted when I wanted. I took the Broadway/Tremont Street MTA bus from the City Point terminal at P and 2nd Street and usually got off at the G Street stop to go to the high school each morning, but when the spirit moved me, I simply stayed on the bus and went into downtown Boston for a day at the movies. The movie district offered theater after theater. There was the Metropolitan (now called the Wang Center), the RKO Keith Orpheum, the Paramount, and the Pilgrim, which was located in what was to become "The Combat Zone" (a section of Washington Street that the city set aside for strip joints, XXX theaters, and video stores.) The theaters all featured a double bill, usually consisting of a major release followed by the previews of coming attractions, a cartoon, and a newsreel preceding another full-length presentation, usually a B movie. The first show was at 9 a.m. but the movies would play continuously until about midnight. I would pick a movie, watch the complete bill, and then go to lunch at Joe and Nemo's, scoff down a couple of hot dogs and a milkshake, and rush back to whichever theater I had decided on to kill the rest of the day before going home as if I had spent a regular day at school. I became an expert on writing notes to the teachers excusing my absences and forging my parents' signatures.

I wasn't there to learn anyway; I was there because the law said I had to be, and I had a desire to play football. Because I had transferred schools, I was ineligible to play varsity football in my sophomore year because of rules put in place to prevent coaches from recruiting kids from other schools to their programs. I played junior varsity in that year and impressed the coaches enough to think I had a good chance to make the varsity starting lineup the following year. Something changed in me when I stepped onto a sports field. My inhibitions melted away, my confidence soared, and I felt I could accomplish anything. Although thin in stature, I had very large thighs, which greatly aided my foot speed and quickness and also gave me surprising strength on the football field. I shocked a number of would-be defenders by running through their arm tackles and breaking a few of their tackles. I also understood the game and had a "nose" for the ball defensively.

I wanted very badly to be on the first team, and when fall practice began, I worked extremely hard. When the starting team was announced, I was named first-string halfback and defensive safety. The euphoria lasted for a couple of days, and within a week I quit the team.

The major flaw in my personality imposed its will once again, and I lost all interest in playing high school football. Just a week before, being on the team was the most important thing in my life, but once the goal was achieved, I could not have cared less. And it wasn't as if I simply lost interest, but I was compelled to quit by something akin to a panic attack, almost claustrophobic in its nature. I *had* to leave the team. Maybe this destructive facet of my personality had something to do with self-loathing. I think it was Groucho Marx who said, "I wouldn't want to belong to a club that would have me as a member." Maybe I could perform as an underdog but couldn't or wouldn't accept the pressure that accompanies high expectations. Maybe I didn't have the inner strength to persevere, to stick it out or to push through. Maybe my flaw was simply lack of discipline. Whatever its root, my failure to finish has dogged me for most of my life.

I didn't return to school for my senior year.

CHAPTER 3

THE CORNER

*T*he world's siren song was beginning to play in stereo. The corner at O and 2nd Streets in the City Point section of South Boston was an island in a sea of trouble. I was at a place in my life where everything was a struggle. My self-confidence was at low tide and still going out. I had suddenly decided to give up trying to be perfect, and now I was going to be like the kids whom I had observed and envied from a distance. There would be no more late nights studying; no more being the outsider because I refused to compromise my values. If I had to do some things that were contrary to my personality in order to fit in, so be it. Here I was finally, unconditionally, accepted; here I became part of a whole, and here my failings were not condemned but commended.

The square, formed by the intersection of O and 2nd Streets, was dedicated to John Joseph Mullen, a local kid who was killed in action in WWI and whose name we appropriated. My family and I were living on East 1st Street, a half block from O and 2nd and adjacent to M Street Park, whose upper level consisted of promenade walks studded with trees and grassy areas and park benches. Facing 1st Street there were tiers of grandstand seats that stretched the entire distance of the park from M Street to N Street and viewed the field below. The area included a baseball and a softball diamond in the summer that converted to a football field in the fall and to ice skating in the winter months. To the right of the N Street end zone stood a clubhouse that separated the football field from a nice Little League diamond and a couple of tennis courts, which were eventually converted to basketball courts (I never witnessed anyone using the tennis courts, at least not for their original purpose), and behind the right-field fence of the Little League park there was a playground for the younger kids with a seesaw and swings.

M Street Park played a big role in a lot of our activities from sports to fighting—and drinking. It was here, on a fall Saturday morning during a pick-up football game, that I met Michael Connolly, who introduced me to the corner and, eventually, to Joe Paulanthony, another good friend.

The thing I liked most about belonging to this group was the simplicity of the rules—and there were rules, rules that most of us believed in and followed and whose breaking had real consequences—the worst of which was losing the trust of your friends. The code was: you always had your friends back, and you never let him take a beating from anyone not from the corner. I recall one instance of a friend having a prearranged fight in M Street Park, and there were only three of us from the corner there, while the other kid had eight or nine friends with him. Our guy started to take a pretty good beating, so we, without hesitation, jumped in and immediately got pummeled by the nine kids from the other side. Losing a fight wasn't a problem; the problem would have been had we not helped our friend. In fact, any battle scars incurred were like a badge of honor, and it was sort of disappointing when they healed. Another rule was never, ever squeal (inform) on anybody, and that meant *anybody*, on or off the corner. The third cardinal rule was to treat your friends with respect. Never steal from them, date their girl, lie to them, or do anything, in general, that might be considered underhanded. You could do what you wanted to an outsider, but not to a friend.

As much as I wanted to belong to this group of kids, I usually became close to one or two guys at a time. I still felt uneasy being with a large group. I guess I've always been somewhat of a loner. I didn't like being at the mercy of other people's actions. If a friend started some kind of trouble, there wasn't any alternative but to get involved, and I preferred to pick my own fights. Over the years I had some really close friends. In retrospect, they were all very different personalities but had one important trait in common, a trait I greatly admired: none would ever compromise their values. They stood up for their beliefs without regard to the repercussions. Michael Connolly and Joe Paulanthony introduced me to the corner. Jimmy Lydon and I were inseparable for a couple of years, and, although we haven't been in touch for decades, I think of him a lot. We had some great times together and stood side by side in a number of fights. The following incident sticks in my mind because it typified our reaction to a challenge and the locker- room humor that is only possible between friends.

For many years I avoided most physical confrontations at any cost. Now I sought them out. We used to drink in a bar located near South Station in Boston named Mallows, where we were liked and welcomed, and that was unique in itself because we, the Mullens, were barred from most of the local bars in South Boston. One night, two guys who were in their early twenties came in and, after a couple of drinks, began to give the bartender and the customers, who were mostly old-timers, a hard time. Jimmy and I told them to knock it off, and they reacted by asking us outside. We couldn't get through the door fast enough. When we squared up with the two loudmouths, I snapped off a left jab at the biggest kid while Jimmy hit him with a vicious right hand. The guy went down and he wasn't getting up for awhile. His buddy put his hands over his head like he was being arrested and quickly backed away. We went back into the bar and were treated like heroes. Jimmy was very thin and had a baby face (he later became a big kid), so the customers and the bartender naturally assumed that I had knocked the guy out. I decided to let them hold on to their version of the event and to rag on Jimmy as I described in detail how I had hit the guy with a beautiful left-hook, right-cross combination I had learned while boxing in the Golden Gloves—all lies, of course. Except for calling me a few choice names, Jimmy took it in good humor, especially as they bought us round after round of drinks. Jimmy was a tough, stand- up guy whom I always respected.

I hung around with Jackie Nee and Joe McCarthy a lot, and I closed many a barroom with Donnie McGonagle; then we would find our way to Waldorf's on Broadway or the Supreme Diner for a late-night dinner or an early morning breakfast, according to your point of view. Later on, Roger Kineavey and I became friends, and Roger was the best man at my wedding. As you can see, the corner wasn't a group of guys who all hung together en masse. Kids became close with those with whom they had the most in common and spent a lot of time with friends of their own choosing. About the only time we were together as a whole was when there was trouble.

The three main activities of life on the corner were sports, fighting, and later on drinking; not necessarily in that order, nor was one exclusive of the others. On many occasions we managed to combine all three.

Sports: We played organized games of football and baseball, either by challenging other corners to a game or through the aegis of the City of Boston Recreation and Parks Department which formed leagues in both sports based on age, supplied the referees and umpires, and maintained the playing fields. But the great games were the ones we created and played on the streets.

I wore out the soles of dozens of shoes by playing our games on the blacktop; sometimes a pair in less than a week. After tiring of stuffing cardboard in my shoe to cover the hole in its sole, only to have the cardboard wear out in the matter of an hour, and not daring to inform my parents that I needed a new pair of shoes once again, I would make a visit to Filene's Basement. Filene's Basement was located on Washington Street in downtown Boston, only a short subway ride from Southie. A section of the basement was dedicated to bins of shoes. The merchandise was usually "seconds" (flawed) and sold at a bargain price. The shoes would be tied together with a piece of twine strung through a hole punched through the side of each shoe so that the pair wouldn't become separated. I would rummage through the bins until I found a pair that struck my fancy and find an empty chair, ostensibly to try on the shoes. After putting on the new shoes, I would cut the twine and use it to attach the old pair together, using the holes remaining from my last "swap." I then placed into the bin the shoes I was wearing when I walked in and walked out wearing the new pair. This was a time long before surveillance cameras.

In the spring and summer, we played a game we called "scrub." The game employed the basic rules of baseball, but was played without a pitcher or a bat. The playing field was on O Street with a manhole cover serving as home plate, the corner of 2nd Street as first base, another manhole cover further up O Street as second base, and the opposite corner of 2nd Street as third. Left field was an empty lot, center field was directly down O Street, and right field was a building that housed a neighborhood store. The ball was a hollow rubber ball filled with air and roughly the size of a baseball. It was called a "pimple" ball because instead of being smooth, its surface consisted of raised bumps. There could be as many as five or six players to a side with each playing various defensive positions, depending on the tendency of the batter. The best athlete, however, played catcher. The batter would stand at home plate, toss the ball into the air, and punch it, much like a serve in tennis, but without the racquet. If the ball wasn't caught in the air, the fielder would throw the ball to the catcher, who would call out the base toward which the runner was heading, and if the catcher named the base before it was reached by the runner, he was out. We used the pimple ball for a number of street games, like "off the step" and "stickball," and, after it had lost its bounce, we would cut it in half and play "half ball," where you would fling the ball to the batter, who would try and hit it with a broomstick.

In the fall and winter, we played "tag rush" in the street or in right field of the Little League diamond at M Street Park from morning until night. Tag rush was played under football rules, except tagging the runner replaced tackling him, but blocking was allowed, which meant a lot of body contact. Those games became quite heated; I've seen teeth knocked out by elbows (the act was usually not inadvertent). I've seen and been the victim of low-bridging defenders taking out a pass catcher's legs, causing a head-first collision with the street, and I've seen fistfights breaking out over whether the ball carrier was tagged or not.

I recall one extremely competitive tag rush game whose score was tied as the last of the daylight was fading. On the last play of the game, I went past the defender as the quarterback heaved the ball as far as he could, and, as I sprinted to get to the ball, I saw a pair of headlights bearing down on me. I had time to get out of the vehicle's path, but, since it was the final play of the game, I decided to go for the catch, since to score the winning touchdown was certainly much more important than being run over by a car. The ball and the car arrived at about the same time, and, as I caught the ball, I leaped as high as I could, hoping to land on the car's hood upright; however, the grill of the car clipped my left foot, flipping me onto the hood, causing me to roll over the windshield to the roof, where I did a half turn, landing on the automobile's trunk in a sitting position, and slid off the trunk, landing on my feet, and continued into the end zone, scoring the winning touchdown. Not quite. The opposing team disputed the touchdown on the grounds that the car was in their way and prevented them from tagging me. That's an example of how serious these games became and an early insight into our mindsets and where our competitive attitudes could and did lead us.

As an aside, our corner had a number of really good athletes. Probably the best was Bobby "Chicken" Noonan, who was an excellent softball fast-pitch pitcher and an even better football player; one of the best defensive players I ever had the pleasure to see. Michael "Oscar" Kineavy was a great, shifty running back; Jackie Conley was a good football player who could fly; Eamon Connolly was a really good pass-catching end with good hands; Thomas "Bobo" Connolly was an excellent shortstop in baseball and softball; Bobby Dunkel was an unbelievable baseball and softball power hitter; Tommy Lyons was an excellent all-around athlete who was a professional ten-pin bowler for awhile; Tom King was a good fullback and a really good power hitter in softball. The list goes on. But even the guys with lesser talent could beat you with their desire and will to win. Hanging on that corner was one big, continuous competition. Some of us used that will to win to our advantage, and for some of us it contributed to our downfall.

Fighting: Fist fighting in the 1950s and 1960s was not only condoned but expected. Everyone accepted fighting as an integral aspect of the ethos of our community, and when I say everyone, I mean everyone—from our peers and our parents to the police. It defined who we were to ourselves and, more importantly, to our friends and family. It didn't matter if you won or lost, only that you fought; that you couldn't be intimidated and would stand your ground, although being good with your hands added a certain cachet to your reputation and did buy you a little more respect when things got tight. And it wasn't just the neighborhood that reinforced this moral code; the movies, radio and television, the novels, and the newspapers of the day extolled the virtue of the lone man facing tough odds by risking everything for the sake of his honor. They stressed the necessity to always standup to every difficult situation, that cowardice was unacceptable, and courage was to be valued above all. Is it any wonder that our generation grew up with a mandate that demanded we display physical courage no matter the risk?

I have been involved in fights when the police happened by to separate the combatants, only to send the winner home and the loser to the emergency room. Identical circumstances today most probably would result in an arrest and possible prison time for the victor. Times and the rules have changed, perhaps not for the better.

Fighting was a rite of passage, and most of us would rank the memory of our first fight right up there with our first sexual experience, our first job, or our wedding. In reality most fights ended with very little physical damage, and the adversaries quickly resumed their friendships.

My first serious fight was with a friend, Arthur Spacone, a kid from the corner and one of the few Mullens who didn't have an Irish surname. We met in an empty lot (left field for our scrub games) after school one day. The fiasco, for me, began as I threw two quick punches, a left hook and right cross, both of which missed their target and were immediately followed by a flurry of punches from Arthur that connected solidly with various points on my face. The "fight" was over in a matter of seconds, leaving me with swelling eyes and a fractured nose. The shame of the loss hurt much more than the blows, and I vowed never to lose like that again. Unfortunately, that wasn't the only promise I wouldn't be able to keep.

The summer months were filled with confrontations. A week didn't pass when there wasn't at least one fight. Someone always had a beef with someone: a kid from the corner, a kid from another corner, or even a complete stranger. We were attracted to places of potential trouble like bees to honey.

One venue that offered a number of opportunities to brawl was "Irish Night." Irish Night was held one evening a week on Castle Island and was meant for Irish families to spend a quiet summer evening celebrating their culture by listening to Irish music being played on loud-speakers or by an occasional live singer and/or step dancers, while being cooled by a gentle breeze wafting off the salt water of Pleasure Bay. This was the atmosphere before we began to attend the festivities. On one such night (I guess I was twelve or thirteen), I saw firsthand where unchecked violence might lead. Eight or ten of the big kids were there when a group of "greenhorns" arrived. Greenhorns were young Irish guys who were born in Ire-land and immigrated to the States. Within minutes the two groups were going at each other, with the Irish kids grudgingly retreating toward an old pier that jutted out into the bay. It soon turned into a full-fledged rout, with the Irish kids leaping into the water and swimming to the safety of a beach about a hundred yards distant. While the big kids were congratulating themselves on their victory, a voice crying out for help could be heard from the end of the dilapidated pier. One of the Irish kids was in the water and hugging a piling for all he was worth, while pleading for help because he couldn't swim. His panic was evident and he was beginning to swallow a lot of water as the swells washed over him. I watched as Buddy Leonard went out onto the pier, and, thinking he was going to the kid's aid, I was shocked to see Buddy wrap his garrison belt (a wide, heavy, leather belt with a large, square, brass buckle) around his right hand so that the buckle swung loose from six inches of leather and begin to pummel the kid's hands with blow after blow until he began to slowly lose his grip and slip into the water. His life was saved only because two men who were there with their families dove into the bay, pulled him from the water, and escorted him to the MTA terminal, eventually putting him on a bus to safety. This was a watershed moment for me because I could sense where our attraction to violence was probably leading us and, although it frightened me, I embraced it.

Another great place to win friends and influence people was the "Moonlight Cruise," which was the 1950s version of today's booze cruise. A large excursion boat would set out from Boston's Rowes Wharf in early evening and sail to Nantasket Beach, an amusement park located south of Boston, where the passengers would disembark to spend a couple of hours in the park doing whatever people do in such places and then re-board the boat for the cruise back to Boston, arriving about 11:30 p.m. The time on the boat was spent drinking and being stimulated by early rock and roll music. By the way, don't let anyone ever tell you that music doesn't have any adverse effects on teenage kids. If I'm any example, that music infected me with both violence and sexual desire. I remember coming out of a movie theater after viewing *Blackboard Jungle*, whose theme song was "Rock Around the Clock" by Bill Haley and the Comets, and wanting to fight someone—anyone. I felt I couldn't contain the energy which that music had incited in me, and, not finding anyone to pick a fight with, I put my fist through the window of a house I was walking past. I spent the next couple of hours waiting to receive stitches in my hand in the Boston City Hospital emergency ward.

The music on the cruise was beginning to affect about forty other kids in much the same manner as it had me. This particular night contained all the necessary ingredients of a formula for disaster. The boat was loaded, in more ways than one, with young, intoxicated, testosterone-filled males from South Boston, rubbing elbows with guys who hung on different corners and with whom they already had a history of contention. By some small miracle, the fight didn't break out until the boat docked and we had disembarked. I can't recall the spark that set off the fight—probably the booze and the music was enough—but Richie Madden and I threw the first punches. Richie hung out on Old Colony Avenue, and we had a little history from having played football against each other. Somehow, however, Davey Connolly and I became paired up (Davey lived on Broadway in City Point but hung out on Old Colony Avenue), and what I remember most about the fight was not its violence, but its length. There were about fourteen different fights going on at once. They began on Atlantic Avenue and, forty-five minutes later, petered out on Summer Street in front of South Station, a distance of about two miles. Davey and I went after each other on four or five occasions with time-outs taken to vomit and catch our breaths, and then we squared off again. I don't think either of us landed more than three punches. In later years Davey and I became friendly, and, as I look back, this was the last man-to-man gang fight I was involved in. From this point on weapons began to creep into the altercations, making them more and more dangerous, and one-on-one fights became more and more rare.

I always had this thought that God put us together with the bullies of the world to teach them a lesson. This is one such encounter. Joe Paulanthony, Bobby Canavan, and I planned a quiet, relaxing weekend in Falmouth on Cape Cod. At the time Falmouth was a party town that drew young people from the Boston area for its beaches and its nightclubs. We left South Boston on a Friday afternoon, drove to Falmouth, and checked into a bed and breakfast. After unpacking, we went out to get a bite to eat and then settled into a local nightclub for a night of drinking.

After ordering three beers, we were sitting in a booth when a girl we knew from South Boston joined us. She was quickly followed by a local guy who sat down beside her, put his arm around her, and tried to kiss her. She began to protest his advances, and we asked the guy to leave her alone; actually we told him to "screw." He jumped up, reached across Joe, and tried to grab me by the throat. Unable to get to my feet because of the booth and the table, I smashed a beer bottle over his forehead (my first beer, by the way), opening a V-shaped gash that began gushing blood. He staggered back onto the dance floor as I pursued him and connected with a flurry of punches as two bouncers who worked for the nightclub grabbed me by each arm, lifted me off my feet, carried me to a telephone booth, and closed and held the door shut as the local police were called. I was taken to the police station and booked on a charge of assault with a deadly weapon. During the booking procedure I slipped my wallet into my shoe, since it contained my actual name and age (I was nineteen, below the legal drinking age), and gave my name as Martin Keough, who was a former Boston Red Sox outfielder. I was held over the weekend to appear in court on Monday morning. On Saturday morning the on-duty police sergeant interviewed me, and, as it turned out, he was from Chelsea, Massachusetts, the city where I was born. We even knew some of the same people. As God would have it, the sergeant reduced the charge to simple assault, eliminating the possibility of me being held pending bail, and indicated the "victim" probably wouldn't testify because of his record and reputation with the local courts based on a number of arrests on similar charges. When I was brought into the courtroom on Monday morning, I was amused to see the room packed with kids from South Boston; some were there as defendants and some as friends of defendants.

As I waited for my case to be called, I was sure it would quickly be dismissed, because the only witness was the instigator who tried to strangle me and he, surely, wouldn't appear. When my case came up the first person called, you guessed it, was my adversary, looking like the fife player in *The Spirit of '76* painting, with a bandage wrapped completely around his head and a black eye. He testified that my attack on him was entirely unprovoked and that he never saw me until I hit him with a bottle. Needless to say I was found guilty and fined fifty dollars. I relate this incident to illustrate a couple of points: first, the lenient treatment I received from the police and the court underscores the attitude of society in those years toward fighting. I'm afraid to think what the penalty would be today for a similar felony, but I know it would have been a great deal harsher than a fifty-dollar fine. Second, this was the first time I used a weapon in a fight—it wouldn't be the last.

On one sultry, summer afternoon, when the mood wavered between contentment and boredom, there were about ten of us talking, tossing a ball around, or just hanging around the corner. However, one of the great things of being part of our gang was circumstances could dramatically change in the blink of an eye, and this was one of those days. A kid from the corner, Ossie, approached us looking visibly upset. He explained that he had sold some "hot" merchandise (the stolen goods were heating bulbs used by auto body repair men to dry new paint jobs) to an auto repair shop owner who told Ossie to come back that afternoon to be paid. When Ossie showed up as they had agreed, the owner refused to pay him and threw him out of the shop. This guy didn't realize it yet, but we never allowed any one of us to be abused in any way without retaliating, and the retaliation was always physical. We not only wanted to avenge our friend's loss and embarrassment, but to not do so would show a weakness in us as a group, and the last thing we were was weak. We immediately piled into a couple of cars and headed to the garage that was located on K Street between Broadway and Third Street. I don't recall everyone who was with us, but I know Paulie McGonagle, Buddy Leonard, Chicken Noonan, Jimmy Lydon, Joe Paulanthony, Ossie, and I were there, along with four or five others. Anyway, we drove the cars onto the sidewalk and rushed into the shop, where three guys were doing whatever they did there. Two of them were quickly knocked down and were being pummeled by baseball bats, tire irons and car antennas. By the way, car antennas became an interesting weapon because you didn't have to carry them with you; when you arrived at the site of a fight, you simply snapped them off the nearest automobile, and, because they had an accordion feature, their length could be adjusted to become an offensive or defensive weapon. The third guy, in fact the one who refused to pay Ossie, ran into a small office area, locked the door, and began to call the police. We quickly broke in the door, ripped the phone out of the wall, and commenced his beating.

Since there were only three of them and we were in such a small space, there wasn't enough room for all of us to get involved with the actual assaults, so we turned on two automobiles that were in the shop for repairs. We smashed their windshields, doors, and rear windows and punctured all eight tires. By now the three guys were unconscious and the cars were wrecked, so it seemed there wasn't much left to accomplish. Not quite. When we were filing out of the shop, I happened to glance back and saw Ossie at the rear wall trying to light on fire sheets of oil-stained burlap that lined the walls. Fortunately the burlap wouldn't ignite, and we got out of there without any fatalities. All of this mayhem over light bulbs.

The Ship's Galley was a bar on Summer Street known as a place to frequent if you wanted a beer and a beating. We began to hang out there because we had worn out our welcome and had been barred from most of the bars in South Boston. The Galley was located a short distance from the Army Base Pier and was home port for the aircraft carrier *Wasp*. When it docked, after what must have seemed an eternity at sea, hundreds of sailors would disembark on their first weekend pass in months, and the first barroom they would encounter on the way into Boston was the Ship's Galley. We were in there every night, and when the sailors—or "swabbies," as we called them—arrived, it wasn't long before things turned ugly. The screech of chairs being pushed back and the crash of tables being knocked over signaled the onset of another donnybrook. The bartender was an army sergeant who worked in the bar as a second job and, after the fights, would bring out his first aid kit and save us hours of waiting in the emergency ward of the Boston City Hospital by stitching up various facial and scalp wounds received in the fracas. There were so many of these brawls that the navy eventually declared the Ship's Galley off limits.

It got worse: within a couple of years, people were shooting each other.

Drinking: My drinking began when I was about thirteen years old. I was a shy, introverted, overly sensitive kid, and I discovered alcohol allowed me to be like the kids I admired most: those who were outgoing, and witty, and cool. When I drank, I felt my anxiety literally melt away, and I could actually have fun and not care how others perceived me. When I got a buzz on, it was as if I became my real self and ceased playing a part that I wrote and acted out for the benefit of the crowd. That was the beneficial side of alcohol's effect. The problem was not only did my anxiety dissolve, but my self-control evaporated with it. I would guess that 90% of the things I did of which I'm ashamed were carried out under the influence of alcohol.

We would begin drinking on Friday evening, and, with the aid of diet pills— Benzedrine or, as we affectionately called them, "Bennies"— we partied until late Sunday night. We would become intoxicated from the alcohol, swallow a couple of Bennies, which would sober us up, and begin drinking again. Bennies served the same purpose and were the fifties version of the Roman vomitoriums without the mess. Alcohol was an important ingredient in my life during this period, and yet I didn't like its taste or the loss of control its use created, but I loved the freedom it gave me. Without it, I hardly spoke in the company of more than two people, and I was more than uncomfortable in any social setting. But when under its influence, I could almost function as a normal person. I could be humorous and intelligent and fit in with a group who actually liked me—or, at the very least, liked the person who was released by the effects of the alcohol.

We mostly drank beer in those days, beer that we obtained (being underage) by giving a street person a dollar to purchase what we needed, and then we'd go to either M Street Park, down the Point (a large, grassy area across the street from Pleasure Bay), or our favorite place, "over the wall," to party. The wall was across 1st Street from the football field at M Street Park that enclosed a large tract of land owned by the Boston Edison Company. It was about six feet high, made of a rough concrete, and stretched along 1st Street almost to L Street. One of us would shimmy to the top of the wall and would be handed the bag of beer and drop to the ground. The ground on the Edison side of the wall was a couple of feet higher, and the descent was a lot easier than the climb. Boston Edison had long since stopped using this part of the grounds, and we had the place to ourselves. It provided a place that was free of any disturbance from the police, girlfriends, or parents. The ground was strewn with old-fashioned cobblestones that we placed in a circle and used as seats and, on at least one occasion, as a potential deadly weapon.

We played a drinking game called "Bizz-Buzz." The rules went like this: the players sat in a circle, and the first person would call out number one; going clockwise, the next player would say two. This would continue around the circle until any number that contained three or five or was divisible by three and/or five. Any player whose turn contained a three or was divisible by a three had to call Bizz, not the number; any player whose turn contained a five or was divisible by a five had to call Buzz, not the number; and any player whose turn contained a three and a five or was divisible by a three and a five had to call Bizz-Buzz. For example, three was Bizz, five was Buzz, and fifteen was Bizz-Buzz. There was even a variation called Bizz-Buzz backward that required the players to switch directions and go counter-clockwise each time a three and/or five came up, only to go clockwise again at the next appearance of three and/or five. Any player who messed up had to chug-a-lug his beer for ten seconds. If you think this game is complicated, try playing after having a few drinks. There were many times we couldn't get by fifteen without an error.

On one beautiful midsummer night, we were over the wall playing Bizz-Buzz, with everyone having a lot of laughs, but as happened frequently with us, the mood turned ugly quickly. Paulie McGonagle and I got into an argument over something to do with the game; I can't recall the details. We got up a couple of times to fight, but cooler heads prevailed, and, thinking the storm had blown over, I sat down to continue the game when Eamon Connolly and Bill Lee jumped up and rushed behind where I was sitting. As I turned, I saw Paulie standing behind me with a cobblestone raised about chest high and trying to bring it down on my head while Eamon and Bill Lee wrestled it from him. Although we made peace that night, needless to say our relationship was never the same, and I developed a habit I have to this day. Whenever I go out to eat or to any number of places, I sit with my back to a section of the room that is least susceptible to a surprise attack. Old habits die hard but they may keep you alive.

Our weekends usually went like this. After supper on Friday nights, we would meet on the corner, get a bag of beer, get drunk, and go to a dance, usually one run by the nuns at the Archbishop Cushing Parochial School on West Broadway. When the dance ended and after walking a girlfriend home, we'd end up on the corner until around midnight and then go home. Saturday was a day of playing sports: baseball in the summer and football in the fall; and Saturday night would bring more drinking and all the craziness the consumption of alcohol precipitated.

Life on the corner bounced back and forth between days of unrelenting boredom to frenetic activity. We could be hanging around doing absolutely nothing and fifteen minutes later, find ourselves facing another gang and fighting for our lives. Even during the times of inactivity, there was always an intensity hanging over me, an anxiety as to what the next hour or day or week might bring. For the first time in my life, I wasn't in control of my actions. I had vowed a total commitment to these kids who had become my friends, but I could see where we were heading and it frightened me. Our anticipation of violence began to escalate as we grew older, and I became addicted to it. Football was an acceptable substitute for gang fights and barroom brawls, but the football season was relatively short and when it ended, brawling was the only activity that could satisfy my craving for physical contact.

When a group of kids—or, for that matter, any age group—bond together as one and adopt a set of rules they believe in and live by, a potentially fatal flaw is created. To cite a current phrase, we had each other's back no matter the situation. It mattered not if our friend was right or wrong; if he had a problem, it was our problem, and we would go as far as needed to back him up. As noble as we felt this posture to be, it led to the eventual downfall for many of our group. When violence is accepted so readily and without recrimination, the ones who are most inclined to violence become leaders and tend to orchestrate the activities of the group simply because the individuals have bought into the all-for-one mind-set. This is true whether the de facto leader is sincere or has simply learned to use the group's commitment to gain his self-satisfying ends.

The acceptance of violence leads to escalating violence, and the corner was far from the only center of conflict. In the coming years there was war in Vietnam, riots in our cities with race and class, and political hatred in every region of our country. I regret my part.

One thing I will never regret is my years on the corner and the kids with whom I grew up, and whom I will never forget and will always love.

CHAPTER 4

NO RETREAT

$\mathcal{T}$ he situation in Southie began to heat-up in the late 1960s and early 1970s as the Mullen gang began to threaten the Killeen brothers' autonomy in the town's illegal activities. Donald, Kenneth, and Edward Killeen ran the bookmaking and loan sharking in South Boston for the last twenty years while the Mullens were mainly thieves whose specialty was stealing goods from warehouses situated along the waterfront and from trucks containing any goods with a quick sale potential. The Mullens, although loosely organized, were independent, young and tough. It was only a matter of time before the two groups clashed.

One night in 1971, the inevitable happened. Mickey Dwyer, a member of the Mullen gang, and Kenneth Killeen got into a fist-fight outside The Transit Café (the Killeen's headquarters) on West Broadway. Mickey, who was an ex-professional boxer, was getting the best of the action until Killeen bit off his nose. When a number of Mullens showed up at the Transit to confront the brothers who had left the scene, Donald Killeen considered it a direct challenge and the war was on.

Our creed of violence had gradually, but inexorably, escalated full cycle from fist fights to gang fights, to fights with baseball bats, car aerials and saps and now, finally, to the use of the ultimate weapons—guns. How could it be otherwise? Is it not a foregone conclusion that if you are taught since your earliest memory to never back down from anyone or anything, and the only way to resolve a dispute is by confrontation and violence, aren't your choices then not just limited but eliminated?

I had escaped the corner years ago by this time, but I observed the consequences of the war, and its aftermath, with great sadness and regret. Many of the victims were my friends and some were like family to me. Had I remained on the corner, the chances were slim or none that I would have been involved in the war with the Killeens, because I don't think I was capable of shooting anyone, but with every new killing, I felt a pang of guilt for deserting my friends. Old values die hard, and if I had stayed, maybe I could have convinced one friend not to participate, and he might be alive today. It seemed as if the whole world had gone mad.

A few weeks after the Mickey Dwyer/Kenneth Killeen incident, "Buddy" Roache (a Mullen) was in the Colonial Room bar at the corner of West Broadway and Dorchester Street when an argument ensued with Whitey Bulger and another Killeen guy, Billy O'Sullivan. "Buddy" was shot and paralyzed for life.

A short time later, one of my best friends was mistaken for his brother and shot to death. Donnie McGonagle had been in the hospital for a diabetic problem for a week or so, and his brother Paulie McGonagle had been using his car. Whitey Bulger recognized the car, pulled up beside it, and shot Donnie to death thinking he was Paulie.

Donnie was one of the good guys. We were very close for a couple of years and had some great times together. Although he was diabetic, his disease didn't prevent us from drinking three or four nights a week, nor from eating all the wrong foods in some all-night diner at three o'clock in the morning after the bars had closed. Donnie could handle himself, but he never went looking for trouble, and he was always a gentleman. Whenever I think of Donnie, two memories immediately come to mind.

The first of which was his flair for the dramatic. We would spend most summer days at the beach, either locally at Pleasure Bay in Southie, or on Cape Cod, or anywhere in between. After we had selected a site to place our blanket, Donnie would run at full speed towards the shore and launch himself into a beautiful dive that would culminate in a belly flop landing a full two feet short of the water. The other beach goers who witnessed his antic would let out an audible gasp, until they realized it was only an act, and then they would applaud.

The other thing I will never forget, was when Donnie had his jaw broken in a bar fight. The doctors wired his jaw shut and the only foods he could swallow were liquids, because of his inability to chew. Since alcohol was liquid, it didn't stop Donnie from drinking his vodka and orange juice through a straw, but as the weeks went by, he was desperate for solid food. We were in the "Ship's Galley" on Summer Street one night and Donnie ordered a plate of Frankfurt and beans. He proceeded to cut the Frankfurt into pieces small enough to fit between his clenched teeth and to slice the beans into quarters with the skill of a surgeon. He then inserted a piece of Frankfurt and a quarter of a bean into his mouth using his tongue to reduce the already infinitesimal bits of food by mashing them against the roof of his mouth and swallowed. This procedure was repeated with the solemnity of a religious ritual for nearly an hour until the plate was empty and Donnie leaned back in the booth with a look on his face of either great satisfaction, or complete exhaustion from the effort.

Donnie's death affected me greatly.

When the Mullens killed Billy O'Sullivan and, in 1972, Donald Killeen; Whitey Bulger inherited the Killeen interests. A meeting was arranged with Pat Nee representing the Mullens and Whitey the Killeen faction. Howie Winter of the Winter Hill Gang and Joe Russo of the Patriaca crime family were the mediators. After the meeting, the two gangs merged with Howie Winter as overall boss. Having known some of the players involved, it wasn't exactly a marriage made in heaven.

In September 1974, court-mandated school busing came into effect causing widespread unrest and violence, especially in South Boston and Charlestown. [2] "Police had to escort and unload buses at several Boston high schools every morning and afternoon, while snipers stood guard on the surrounding rooftops. Metal detectors were installed and troopers patrolled the cafeterias, hallways and stairwells, and still racial brawls broke out daily. Federal Judge Garrity also ordered equal numbers of black and white police officers to guard the schools, provoking racial hostility even within the police force. "It'll be lucky if the Boston police don't kill each other before the day is out," said one state trooper at the time. For three years, as many as 300 state police officers a day, patrolled South Boston High. One teacher compared the school to a prison: "We can't leave school; we can't come early or on the weekends to do preparatory work. We are like prisoners. Every day when I get up, it's like getting up to go to prison."

[2]Reference *Hoover Institution-Policy Review No. 92* entitled *Busing's Boston Massacre*

Given the circumstances this generation endured each day there was little or no chance they would be the one to break this ever-expanding circle of violence.

In late 1974, another friend was shot to death. Paulie McGonagle was killed by Whitey Bulger and another individual alleged to be Tom King [3] (the same Tom King my mother wanted me to spend more time with) after being lured into an automobile by Whitey with a ruse[4]. We were very friendly for a number of years but we had a falling out and our relationship was never the same[5]. Paulie was a unique character, who was always planning his next scam. He was an expert at passing counterfeit bills and in the use of stolen credit cards. He was using a credit card stolen from a female whose name was Michelle something or other, and convinced the store clerk that he was French Canadian and that the name on the card was actually Michael in French. Even when he was a young kid, he was unpredictable. We played this game called *Relievio* whose object was to capture everyone on the other team. As their hiding places were discovered, they would be led to the stoop of a tenement building and held captive by one opponent, until either everyone was captured, or they were freed by someone on their team who was able to gain the stoop and shout "relievio". On one night, Paulie stole a car; drove onto the sidewalk, jumped out and freed his team. On another night he simply went home and left us searching for him for over an hour.

He was caught driving a stolen car one night when he was about sixteen years old. He feigned being crippled and told the police officers he was suffering from polio and was in a lot of pain. The police drove him to the Boston

[3] Reference *Brutal* by Kevin Weeks and Phyllis Karas
[4] See Chapter 8, The Other Guy
[5] See Chapter 3, The Corner

City Hospital for medical attention and as one officer went for a wheelchair, Paulie ran into the South End alleyways and escaped.

Years later, Paulie and four other kids from the corner broke into a drug store in Brookline. A beat policeman happened by and shots were fired. The guys managed to get to their car but were stopped by police a couple of miles away and only Paulie escaped by fleeing on foot. He was later arrested but found not guilty in a subsequent trial.

He seemed to lead a charmed life. But if it was charmed, his luck ran out when he went missing in late 1974. His car and wallet were found along the Charles River and the story for public consumption was: "that he was killed by relatives of a girlfriend for abusing her." His body was uncovered decades later in a shallow grave on Tenean Beach in Dorchester.

Tom King was complex, to say the least. We had some interesting, intelligent conversations when he was sober. But when he was under the influence of drugs or alcohol, I would avoid him like the plague. He could turn in a moment from a real gentleman into a very dangerous individual. One night, he and I were in the Triple O's bar just talking, when a local woman who had more than enough to drink began to belittle Tom about something or other. He ignored it for a minute or two and then without a word walked over to her and hit her with a right hand punch that knocked her unconscious before she hit the ground. He then went to the telephone and called the owner of the bar, Kevin O'Neil, to tell him what had happened. Kevin's reply was "when she wakes up tell her she's barred".

Tom was a very good athlete. In fact, the first time I met him was on the athletic field. Unfortunately for him, it had to be a home game, because he played for Walpole State Prison. I played for a team in the Boston Park League and Walpole was on our schedule and, although we didn't know each other at the time, I knew who he was. Tom spent a lot of his early years in prison, but I don't recall why he was serving time when we played against each other. A friend of his on the outside asked me to smuggle in a baggie of "black beauties" (Benzedrine). On the first play of the game, I was to tackle the full back (Tom) and while we were on the ground, pass him the baggie. Just before the ball was snapped, I retrieved the baggie from my athletic supporter, made the tackle and handed off the contraband to Tom. Mission accomplished. The Walpole team then went on to annihilate us and I always wondered if they were aided by the chemical boost I had provided.

In November 1975, Tom's temper guaranteed him a place in South Boston's folklore and reinforced, if anyone had a doubt, Whitey's reputation for ferocity. As the story goes, one night at the Triple O's, Tom got into an argument with his wife, that quickly became physical. Whitey stepped in to stop it, and Tom either pushed or grabbed Whitey while warning him not to put his hands on him. Tom soon went missing.

On the same day that Tom disappeared, another friend and Mullen "Buddy Leonard," was found shot to death in a car. The cover story that went around South Boston was that Tom King had killed "Buddy" Leonard and went on the run. The real story was one of the worst kept secrets ever. The truth was being whispered throughout South Boston within days of the incident, which makes me wonder if it was leaked on purpose as a warning to any of Whitey's other potential rivals.

Regardless, the marriage from hell was pretty much dissolved.

This never-back-down attitude that was drilled into us from our earliest age, was not confined to those who chose a life style of crime that inevitably put them in harm's way. We all held courage in high esteem in some form or another, and our corner, in fact Southie, as a town, paid a dear price for overcoming our fear of danger. Of course, nothing is universal, but for the most part, when a Southie kid was faced with a choice of fight or flight; he usually fought.

Joey Desmond was a kid from the corner, who was younger than me, but who I helped coach in football. He was a quiet kid, who loved sports, especially football, and was a pleasure to have on the team. He joined the Marine Corps and was killed-in–action in Viet-Nam.

Donald Turner was a good friend of my brother, in fact; he lived with us in my parents' home for a bit. He was another football player, and was married with a young son. Donald joined the Marine Corps and was killed-in-action in Viet-Nam.

Johnnie Cole was probably my brother's best friend but they were trouble waiting to happen when they were together. For example, Jerry Williams was a local radio call-in talk show host, who is often credited with inventing that genre. He was extremely liberal in his social and political views, and as such he wasn't very popular in South Boston. Each March 17th, Southie would host a Saint Patrick's Day parade, and one year, Mr. Williams was invited to ride in a convertible advertising his radio station and his show. My brother and Johnnie Cole ran alongside Jerry Williams' car and hit him in the face with a pie. From that moment on, Jerry hated South Boston, and for a long period he wouldn't accept calls from there.

Johnnie joined the Marine Corps and was killed-in-action in Viet-Nam. All in all, there were an improbable twenty-five kids from Southie killed in Viet-Nam.

Paulie Lentini, another kid from the corner, was a Lieutenant on the Boston Fire department, and while fighting a fire in the Back Bay, the building collapsed, killing him and another firefighter, James Gibbons, in 1981 long before their time. I wasn't there that night, but I knew Paulie and he wouldn't and didn't hesitate to enter that burning building with his men.

Peter Nee was a respectful, polite gentleman. One night he happened to be with some friends, who became involved in a physical confrontation with three other kids, who all knew each other. The fight would break up and then continue later on during the night. It culminated with Peter being shot to death. What an awful waste of a good human being. Peter could have left his friends and gone home on a number of occasions but to walk away from trouble or to desert your friends was not an option for a Southie kid and it cost him his life.

When our old men want the youth of the country to fight their wars for them they espouse the same values that we in South Boston grew up with: namely loyalty, courage and sacrifice. Yet when these same people observe the town, it is labeled as insular, bigoted and violent. I suppose there is a time and a place for everything but I just can't see how these values can be turned on and off according to the circumstance. They are either truths to be lived by or they are not.

I will admit that the threat of violence pools just below the civility of the town, but it is very few who siphon it to the surface for their own ends. Most confrontations lead to a verbal argument, a shoving match or an inconsequential fist-fight where one or two punches are thrown and it is over. The real violence is committed by those, who for their own motives, took hold of that thread of violence and wove it into a rope—a rope that was used as an instrument of fear and, more importantly, control.

My dilemma has always been between my aversion to confrontations and violence on one side, and my determination to never back down on the other. The latter has always prevailed, as it has for most kids from Southie.

CHAPTER 5

AFTER THE FALL

*T*hings were beginning to spiral out of control. My drinking was getting the best of me. I needed alcohol or at least its effect. It wasn't that I drank every day or couldn't wait for my next drink; its power lay in knowing that it was there for me in those situations where I felt inadequate and unable to join in a social setting. With a couple of drinks, the anxiety would melt away, and at worst, I wouldn't become a "wallflower" and at best, I could be the life of the party. The dilemma was my inability to stop at a couple of drinks. If two drinks changed my personality so miraculously for the better, what would four or five drinks have wrought? Very rarely was I able to drink without becoming intoxicated, and in that altered state of mind, I risked making that one big mistake that could be life-changing.

The violence was escalating to the point where weapons were being used consistently. The rules were changing. Kicking a person who was down or "giving him the boots" was considered dirty fighting only a short time ago. Now if we didn't kick him, we would be chided by our friends for being weak. Baseball bats, clubs, saps (blackjacks), and car aerials became the weapons of choice. One-on-one fights were becoming a thing of the past, and if one of us got into a fight, the rest of us would "jump in" whether there was one guy or twenty on the other side. The adrenalin rush brought on by the violence was starting to become habit-forming, and like a narcotic I needed more and more to maintain the high.

The brawls were breaking out more frequently. We sometimes had two or three melees a week not to mention the occasional one-on-one fistfight. I was introduced to violence on numerous occasions at a very young age, and even though they weren't aimed at me, they were, nevertheless, very traumatic experiences. The first incident occurred when I was about five or six years old, and for whatever reason, my father beat up a guy in our living room. I still recall I had two distinct reactions to the fight. My first emotion was one of horror and fear, but I also felt a surge of pride that my father was capable of protecting us, and I could feel safe living in his house. These distinctly opposite feelings toward violence remained with me for the rest of my fighting life. After a fight and having given someone a beating, I would have an immediate rush of pride for winning that was quickly followed by an attack of conscience and revulsion that lasted for days. So, although I relished the fighting, my motives were probably dissimilar from those of most of my friends. I didn't have any desire to put a beating on anyone. But after years of being bullied and recalling the shame of walking away from a challenge, I wanted to exert my will on whomever I was fighting. I wanted him to know I had beaten him, and if it took one punch or twenty punches, my goal was to force him to surrender his determination to win. By searching the other guy's eyes, I knew within the first ten seconds of a fight how competitive it would be. I could judge if he was beaten before a punch was thrown, or he would battle until one of us was knocked out or too exhausted to continue. One night I squared up to fight a kid who was so intimidated, I declared him the winner and walked away without throwing a punch. Conversely, I've fought guys whom I hit with everything but the kitchen sink and they kept coming. The winner was usually the one who wanted it the most.

Anger began to control me. It was always there, bubbling just below the surface, capable of erupting at any moment, and a great deal of my energy was consumed in the throes of a fit of anger or trying to keep it in check. I loved sports. I loved playing sports and I loved watching sports, but I never enjoyed sports. My persona was inexorably linked to the wins and losses of the Boston professional sports teams, especially the Red Sox and Boston Celtics. The Bruins and the Patriots were included in later years. A loss by one of these teams would put me in a dark mood, and a bad loss would cause me to explode in uncontrollable anger. I have punched walls, tossed radios out of windows, destroyed furniture, and on one occasion put my foot through a television set because a Philadelphia Warrior player (I think it was Hal Greer) hit a half-court shot at the buzzer to beat the Celtics in a playoff game. And even when they won, which the Celtics did with great regularity, the elation of a win was far outshadowed by the despair of a loss.

Football was the only discipline I practiced. It offered me a legitimate outlet for the anger and violence I fought to keep in check. We would practice three or four evenings a week, which sapped a lot of excess energy and took up the time I would have spent consuming alcohol, thus avoiding the negative activities that go hand-in-hand with drinking. On game day, after a couple of hours of blocking, tackling, and being tackled, I was physically and

THE LONG WAY HOME

emotionally spent, and the last thing I wanted was to go out looking for problems. In retrospect, football season was the time of year when I got into the least trouble.

Unfortunately, my intensity on the playing field wrecked any chance of enjoying the competitive nature of the game, and I would do *anything* in my power to win. We were playing a football team from Dorchester in a Boston Park League game one Sunday afternoon. I was a good ball carrier, and if I got by the defensive line and into the opposing team's secondary, it usually resulted in a big gain, if not a touchdown. On this particular day I broke through the defensive line five or six times, but I was tackled each time by the other team's safety. I tried everything. I gave him my best moves. I tried running around him, and I tried running over him—all to no avail. My frustration was building and my anger was beginning to surface. The game was now secondary; this was all about him and me. Late in the game our offensive line opened a huge hole, and avoiding the linebacker on that side, I broke into the secondary with my nemesis five yards to my left and closing fast. I let out a scream of pain and began hopping on my right leg as if I had injured my left knee or ankle. He, having some compassion, broke stride and slowed up just enough for me to accelerate and run by him for what proved to be the winning touchdown. It wasn't bad enough that I had used an underhanded ploy to beat him, but when we lined up for the extra point, I rubbed it in by taunting him with words that I hesitate to repeat. I relate this incident, certainly not to brag; I'm not very proud of it, but to illustrate how far I had fallen from that boy who, not so far in the recent past, would never had resorted to such dishonesty and mean-spirited actions and who wanted only to please God. I'm sure God didn't feel honored by my antics on that day nor on many more days to follow.

Even my "job" was counterproductive. My father worked on Castle Island in South Boston for Wiggins Terminal, an outfit that bought, stored, and sold lumber. He used his influence to get me into the union, and because the work was sporadic, the job was ideal for my new lifestyle. We were hired on a day-to-day basis. Each morning I "faced" a "pick-up" where the men needed for the day would be hired based on their seniority, and since I was new and far down the seniority list, the work rarely lasted more than five days at a time, and then I would be off for a week or more. Perfect! I had some spending money and plenty of time to spend it. Most of my days and nights were free to experiment with my newfound freedom and hedonism.

And then one cold mid-winter's night, I had one of those unexpected watershed moments that we all experience but a few times in our lifetime. I had this mistaken belief that I was some kind of avenging angel whom God used to teach bullies and arrogant people a lesson by punching them around or forcing them to back down. Suddenly I realized that I had become like the very people I despised—I was the arrogant bully. This lesson was clearly brought home to me one night at the old Boston Garden. Three or four of us were at a Celtics game after spending a couple of hours drinking at a local bar. I left my seat to go downstairs to the concession stand to get a beer. As I turned to go back to my seat, a guy bumped into me and spilled the beer all over me. He apologized profusely and offered to buy me another beer, but I would have none of it. One profane word led to another, and we agreed to go outside to settle the problem. The old Garden had these wide, winding, marble stairs that were interrupted by large landings, and as we reached the first landing, I hit him with a sucker punch that drove him into the wall. As I moved in for the knockout, he calmly reached into his pocket, withdrew a handkerchief and positioned it as a mouthpiece to protect his teeth. This wasn't the first time he had been in a situation like this, and I immediately knew I was not facing an easy task. Little did I know how hard it would prove to be. I threw a left-jab, right-hand combination, both of which he easily avoided, and the rest was history. He began to pummel me with lefts and rights to the body, driving me across the landing into the opposite wall. I felt two of my ribs let go on my left side, and the pain was so acute, I couldn't lift my hands to either fight back or even protect myself. At this point my hope was he would finish me, and the fight, and walk away. I tried to slide down to the marble floor of the landing to escape the punishment he was meting out, but he kept me on my feet by the power of his punches to my torso. Finally he hit me with four punches in quick succession that broke my nose, cracked a cheekbone, and blackened both of my eyes. By the time I collected my senses, he was gone and I wasn't sorry.

I learned a great deal about myself that night at the Garden. It was only a few short years past that I was a kid doing my best to live up to an all-encompassing moral code, the core of which was to follow the word of God. As I studied the events of that night at the Garden, I wondered where I had gone and who I had become. Was I, in reality, the person who had become addicted to violence and alcohol, who went about seeking my next fix no matter who got hurt? The physical beating itself had little or no bearing on my thoughts; physical pain had no effect on me except to curtail my activities until I healed. The real pain was the disgust I felt for myself because of who I had allowed myself to become.

I wish I was able to say this was my final fight, but it wasn't. It was, however, the last time I provoked a confrontation, and from that night on I avoided situations that I knew would lead to violence as often as possible without risking the loss of my friends' trust. I wasn't able to quit my addiction "cold turkey," but I knew I had to wean myself from the high of physical combat.

I was rapidly approaching a point of no return. Something had to change.

The author before the "fall" ...

And after the "fall"

The author with Bobby Cummings (seated) taken during "Quiz Down" radio show. We were friendly rivals throughout grammar school. Bobby was tragically killed in an airplane crash.

The John Joseph Mullen memorial sign at the corner of "O" and 2nd streets. We appropriated the Mullen name as the name of our gang. He was killed in action in the Korean conflict.

The author today on the corner of "O" and 2nd streets...
where it all began.

The house at 19 "O" Street where the author lived
during his formative years.

"M" Street Park (officially called Christopher Lee Playground) where we played sports, drank, and dated.

Castle Island (today) where the Irish Nights were held in the 1950s.

Our wall on 1st street hasn't changed from the 1950's when it was
our sanctuary and drinking place.

The nation's first Viet-Nam Memorial erected in South Boston.

The author's liquor store with its ill-conceived
shamrock building decor.

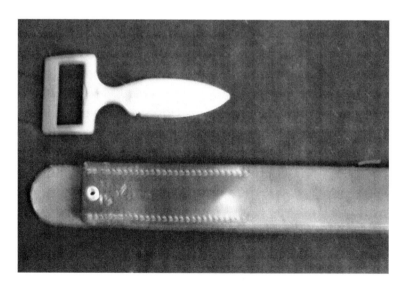

One of the many gifts "Whitey" presented me.
When this belt buckle is removed it becomes a knife.

CHAPTER 6

CHASING AFTER THE WIND

*T*he incident at the Boston Garden planted a seed, and it began to take root. The time was coming to move on with my life. I had met and fallen in love with Peggy Gunn. She awoke within me a sense of normalcy, a sense that life on the corner couldn't sustain itself in the long run without ending in disaster. Some of my friends were getting into heavy crime; the fights were becoming more violent, and the use of weapons becoming more commonplace. My drinking wasn't getting any better, and I realized a total change in direction was required if I was ever going to lead any semblance of a productive life.

Peggy and I decided to get married. We were only eighteen and nineteen years old, respectively, and the assumption of everyone, from our parents to the priest who was to perform the ceremony, was that Peggy was pregnant. She wasn't. But, afraid of the answer, no one asked us the question. It was a pretty scary time for both of us. I didn't have a steady job, and there weren't any possibilities in sight. Peggy was working, but in the early sixties, the man was expected to provide for the family and the woman was to run the household and raise the kids, and I intended to continue that way of life with my family. We had settled on a small wedding with just the immediate family in attendance, but our parents had a meeting and decided to extend the immediate family to about two hundred people. Of course neither family had the money to afford such a large wedding, so most of the burden fell on us to finance the wedding reception.

The biggest obstacle to our marriage was my divorce from the corner. The only chance we had was for me to make a complete break with my friends and the lifestyle I had come to cherish. I had observed others who tried to balance marriage while holding onto life on the corner and it just couldn't work. The corner was family and for a marriage to survive, a man must leave his father and mother, his friends, and anything or anyone else who might be an obstacle to a complete commitment to his wife, and the two should become one. I knew this to be truth even before I knew it to be God's plan for a man and woman, and I set about to make it happen. For a couple of months before our wedding date, I stopped hanging on the corner and quit drinking and began spending more time with Peggy. I was determined to be a good husband and, eventually, a good father, but I was filled with doubt and trepidation. My track record for perseverance was sketchy, at best. I was still working at Wiggins, which was virtually part time; I had no education, not even a high school diploma; and the idea that I would be responsible for a wife and, most likely, kids scared me half to death. I wasn't sure I was capable of taking care of myself, let alone a family, and I vacillated between the anticipation of a new beginning and fear of the unknown.

By concentrating on the immediate details necessary to put together our wedding, the reception, our honeymoon, and a place for us to live, I was able to focus on the present and couldn't dwell on the uncertainty of the future. About a month before the wedding, we rented a small apartment on Story Street across the street from South Boston High, and we were able to acquire a suite of furniture, dishes, silverware, and whatever else was necessary to set up housekeeping. The rent for the apartment was about $35 a month, and we bought our furniture on a payment plan. We didn't have an automobile, a telephone, a clothes washer, or a dryer, nor did we think them necessary.

The day finally arrived. It was late June, the 23rd, and the day dawned sunny and pleasant. I rose early, went into the bathroom, shaved, and gave myself a haircut. When my father saw what I had done, he immediately began to berate me for being so stupid as to cut my own hair on the day of my marriage. So the last morning I was to live in his house began, like so many others with he and I butting heads and disagreeing, as was our usual relationship. Nothing changed. The ceremony was scheduled for 10 a.m. at Saint Brigit's Church on Broadway, about a block from our homes (Peggy and I lived directly across 2nd Street from each other). The reception was held at the Marine Park Associates building on East 4th Street at 12 noon. Ironically, the building where our wedding reception was held was formerly Police Station 12, built in 1874, and would once again play host to a large police presence on June 23, 1962.

We were to honeymoon in Dennisport on Cape Cod at a family-owned cottage that was built by my mother's grandfather as a place to live during the summer months while they rented out their house to vacationers. Although the cottage didn't cost anything, it wasn't exactly replete with all the comforts of home. Its lighting was furnished by kerosene lamps; water was supplied by a hand pump;

we cooked on a stove that burned kerosene- soaked wicks that constantly had to be adjusted to control the height of the flame and the most exciting extra convenience of all was that the toilet was an outhouse. My father lent us his car for the week, and as an example of my irresponsibility, I took the test to obtain my license all of four days before our wedding. As luck would have it, I passed and was issued a temporary license, or I would have taken the chance and driven without one. As it was, I don't think I had driven a car more than two or three times in my life. God was still looking out for me.

The wedding ceremony went off without a hitch. We went to have our pictures taken and arrived back at the reception in time to see my father tell some of the younger kids from the corner that they weren't invited and not to try and "crash" the party. These kids were fifteen and sixteen years old, and my father had a strict personal moral code about underage drinking. Anyway, this incident was just the first of many confrontations to occur during the day and, in fact, during the entire weekend. Peggy and I went through the usual rituals associated with wedding receptions, all but the cutting of the cake. We were seated at the wedding party table, and after the various toasts were completed and before the ceremony of the cake cutting was to take place, we were taking a couple of minutes to catch our breath. The three-tier wedding cake was placed on the wedding table just in front of us, and we were to come to the front of the table to complete the cake cutting, and then it was to be removed to a side table to be distributed to the guests.

Just then an older guy from the corner, who was an alcoholic, (or, as we called them back then, a "wino" and today would be labeled a "homeless person") pulled up a chair to the wedding party table opposite Peggy and me, placed a plate of food down, and began to eat. A number of our friends tried to convince him to move, and when he refused, they grabbed hold of the back of his chair and began to slide him away from the table. This proved to be a good idea that quickly went bad, for unbeknownst to them, he had taken hold of the tablecloth with both hands, and, oblivious to the warnings from the few people who were aware of the potential disaster, they pulled harder on the chair. Plates, glasses, silverware, and, most importantly, the wedding cake went crashing to the floor. We weren't married three hours, and already Peggy was in tears, frightened, and embarrassed. I tried to lighten up the situation by telling her we, at least, didn't have to listen to that inane "the bride cuts the cake" song.

We both knew how quickly things would get out of hand, especially with an open bar, and so we had decided weeks ago to escape the inevitable bedlam to come as quickly as possible. As soon as we had performed everything expected of us, we escaped as if fleeing from a bank robbery. The car was already packed. We grabbed the wedding gifts and headed for Cape Cod. As we drove away from the reception, I felt a pang of loss, for I knew I would never again experience the bond I had with the corner and with the guys who were such an important component of my life. I was turning my back on them; I was walking away from the only friends I had ever known and it was painful, but I knew it was my only chance of survival.

The party progressed or regressed, according to individual interpretation. There were a number of fights at the reception, and the people operating the hall had to call the police because everyone refused to leave hours after our rented time had run out. The police backed a paddy wagon up to the door and herded our guests out, using the wagon as a threat. I don't recall if anyone was actually arrested. The moveable feast reconvened on 2nd Street at our parents' houses which were across the street from each other. My friends had taken the liquor from the reception and, on the way to the new party headquarters, had commandeered two construction horses with blinking yellow lights and semi blocked off the street in front of our parents' houses. There were numerous fights, some between my family members and my friends, some between my friends, and some with strangers who were just passing by. The party lasted until Sunday evening.

Meanwhile Peggy and I spent our honeymoon night counting the money given to us as wedding gifts. It was the custom in our social circle to give money rather than presents as a gift. We received over $5,000 in cash, a Hummel, and four IOUs that were never redeemed.

I am always struck by the polar difference between the world's values and those of God. Our society acknowledges such human characteristics as pride, ego, individualism, and the accumulation of riches as traits to esteem in others and to greatly desire for ourselves. Yet, except for a few, very rare instances, God proclaims them to be sins to be assiduously avoided. We need only to see the havoc these "qualities" have unleashed on a world He had designed as perfect to agree with His logic.

But having tried to play by God's rules—or, at least, His rules as I understood them— and then by my own, and having failed at both, I decided, by default, to join society and adopt its values as my own. In keeping with my past performance, I went all in.

I continued to work in the lumberyard and between what I earned there, unemployment insurance, and Peggy's job, we kept our heads above water. In October of 1962, three months after our marriage, I applied for a factory job with the Safety Razor Division of the Gillette

Company and was hired on a temporary or conditional basis with a three-month probationary period. The plant was located in South Boston, a short bus ride from our apartment. My first assignment was in the Foamy (shaving cream) department as a stock clerk whose job was to take the cans of Foamy from the conveyor belt and stack them on pallets to be packaged and shipped to the retail customers.

Gillette was a great place to work. Even though it was a company that had sales in the multi-millions (the company's sales actually hit a billion dollars while I was employed there), it treated its employees as a mom-and-pop organization might. There was a family-like atmosphere where the employee was treated with respect, and anyone in a position of authority who didn't honor the culture was reprimanded or worse. Gillette and the companies like it were the vehicles that helped to create and sustain the middle class in this country. The company provided its employees with a living wage, cost-free comprehensive health insurance, and an in-house medical clinic complete with x-ray machines and lab facilities staffed by full-time nurses and four or five doctors who rotated duty. We had a cafeteria that served a three-course meal, prepared on premises for thirty-five cents, free parking, and a myriad of recreational activities. There was a softball league that played on a beautiful, manicured diamond located on the premises, a horseshoe league, a basketball league, a hockey league, and a bowling league. They even taught fencing for a while. Every activity had a year-end banquet complete with awards, and they had a family day outing at Canobie Lake in New Hampshire every summer.

But the greatest, most valuable benefit Gillette offered was their job posting system. Every non-salaried position that became available was posted on bulletin boards throughout the plant and could be bid on by anyone as long as it was a higher pay grade. In five years I was able to avail myself of the opportunities presented by the program to advance into a number of factory jobs until finally a clerk's position became available in the accounting department. I bid on it and was accepted. I was now an official card-carrying member of the "rat race," and my next twenty years were dedicated to "getting ahead," better known as "making something of myself." When I accepted the accounting clerk's job, I knew I was taking a calculated risk. Because of the overtime and shift differential pay I earned in the factory, I actually took a pay cut to gain entry into the accounting department, hoping the potential in having a profession outweighed the short-term reduction in wages. The roadblock was my lack of education, and so I immediately began taking evening accounting and business courses at Northeastern University in Boston. During some semesters I was attending four classes a week, which required my presence in Boston two or three nights a week after work in addition to spending the weekends studying or doing homework. This workload went on for eight to ten years.

Life at home was going well, and Peggy became pregnant with our son John in the fall of 1963. We moved from Story Street to a third-floor apartment on L Street soon after. The call of the corner was still strong, and although I had quit drinking, I missed the camaraderie and the excitement of O and 2nd Streets. I remember the day that I realized I was really and truly married. I had to empty the dufflel bag that held my football equipment to fill it with our clothes that needed washing at the local Laundromat. As hard as I tried to stay away from the guys and the corner, there were times when I emotionally

75

needed to be there and when offered an excuse, I jumped at the opportunity. I would be invited to participate in a football game or a flag football league that was being organized, or a stag party for someone getting married, or even a fight or two. Another problem was we would get occasional visitors carrying a case of beer, usually after the bars closed at 2 a.m., who wanted to continue the party at our house, not to mention friends who wanted to borrow money. There was a time I would not have denied these guys anything; they were my family. But I knew the decisions I made now were critical to whether our marriage had a chance to succeed, and with the impending birth of our first child, I sensed we had to get out of Southie.

As much as I was tempted and torn between my responsibility to my wife and yet unborn child or the freedom of total irresponsibility, it was settled with the birth of our son, John. When I saw that perfect little human being for the first time, God tore down the barriers I had built and flooded my heart with a love so intense, it was palpable. I didn't know it was possible to love anyone as I loved him. I couldn't wait to be with him after work and on weekends. I was working the 6 a.m. to 2:30 p.m. shift at Gillette, and Peggy would meet me at the bus stop with John in his stroller, and I would take him for a walk until suppertime. On weekends just the two of us would go down to the beach at Pleasure Bay or out to Castle Island on cold winter days with John bundled up in a green winter snowsuit, green hat with ear muffs, and wrapped in a heavy blanket, looking like the little brother in *A Christmas Story* except John didn't have to try to walk which, even if he was capable of doing, would have been impossible, given the many layers of clothes he was bundled up in. As I pushed him in his stroller, I kept him informed on what was happening in my life, even if he didn't understand a word of what I was saying. He was privy to my deepest longings, my likes and dislikes, and most of all I warned him of the pitfalls that life would put in his way and how to avoid them. He was my whole life.

I believe God offers us choices at key points in our lives, and I believe the birth of my son was one of these choices. At my first glimpse of John, God instantly softened my heart and gave me back the ability to feel love and the courage to risk emotional pain. Unfortunately I wasn't able to sustain that courage for long.

About this time my father bought a two-family house in Whitman, a town about thirty miles south of Boston. This was the answer to the two biggest dilemmas I was wrestling with. The first was moving out of South Boston and away from the corner, and the second was getting John away from the physical dangers and temptations inherent in the city. Now I understand that these same problems exist in the suburbs, but I always thought that my life would have been much different if I had grown up in a different environment, and I wanted to give my son that opportunity. Peggy struggled with the move. She missed Southie and her family, and I think she thought of the move as temporary for a long time. We bought a new Chevy Nova, and since Peggy was a relatively new driver and wasn't confident backing up, I would back the car out of the driveway two or three nights a week and point it towards Boston so she could go to play Bingo in Southie.

Our second child, Kellie, was born in Whitman. Well, we lived in Whitman, but she was born in the Boston Lying-In Hospital in the city. Peggy wasn't one to have a long labor period, and we barely made it to the hospital before Kellie made her debut. I remember visiting Peggy the next morning (Kellie was born on Super Bowl I Sunday) and hearing a baby cry. Before having ever seen her, I hadn't a doubt it was Kellie crying. I walked down to the nursery and, sure enough, it was she. That wasn't the last time I would recognize her cry. It was distinctive because she usually cried from anger or frustration more than hurt or hunger. Even as a baby she was strictly her mother's child, and try as I might, she didn't like me very much. She seemed to sense when Peggy was going to Bingo, and on one particular night, as soon as Peggy drove away, Kellie began to cry. It wasn't really crying but more of an angry howl; there were no tears, only the sound of her howl. I tried everything—holding her, feeding her, playing with her, reading her stories—all to no avail, and she kept this going from six o'clock until her mother came home around ten. It became a clash of wills, a competition of sorts to see who would blink first. I finally lost it and began to scream back at her just as Peggy came through the door and accused me of being insane. She went to the crib, and as she picked Kellie up, she immediately stopped crying and boldly turned to me, sporting a broad, self-satisfied grin on her now angelic face. Kellie 1, Dad 0.

On another occasion Kellie began to cry as Peggy was about to leave. When she decided to stay home, I told her to go, regardless of how Kellie was acting. I'd be darned if we were going to allow a two-year-old to dictate how we would live our lives. I picked Kellie up and held her as Peggy left. No sooner had the door closed than Kellie began to hyperventilate, her lips turned purple, her eyes went back into her head, and she fainted. When she passed out she relaxed and was able to exhale, reviving herself. Holding Kellie, I ran out to the driveway to stop Peggy from driving away and handed Kellie over to her, sheepishly mumbling something about her staying home tonight. Kellie 2, Dad 0. She experienced a number of these episodes over a year-and-a-half span. We took her to doctors, but they weren't very concerned about it and predicted she would grow out of it. She did, but it was pretty scary while it lasted.

Outwardly things were going well. I had, for the most part, broken from the corner, and I continued to advance in Gillette. I was achieving a promotion almost every year or year and a half, nothing spectacular, but a steady progression of more responsible positions and salary increases. Beginning as an inventory clerk, I became a finished stock inventory analyst, blade production analyst, new product cost estimator, cost accounting supervisor, and, finally, cost accounting manager. Sometime during these years we were able to purchase our own home that we bought from Peggy's sister in Hanson, a town just south of Whitman. I was living the American dream: a loving wife, two great kids, a career, our own home, and a car. All we were missing was a dog and a station wagon.

But something else *was* missing. I was less and less fulfilled with each passing year. Any satisfaction derived from my promotions quickly dissipated, and the new position simply became just another job. The anxiety I had felt about school as a kid tripled in both the work environment and my college classes at Northeastern. After the softening of my heart when my son was born, I had, once again, retreated into my defensive posture and rebuilt the barrier guarding my heart that John's birth had torn down. The most obvious event that sent me scurrying back to the safety of that secret, private place where I was able to protect my overly sensitive psyche from an increasingly painful world occurred as John became a little older and began to experience his own emotional hurts inherent in the growing-up process. He was being bullied by a couple of the neighborhood kids in Whitman on an ongoing basis, and as I observed the harassment he was receiving, the pain of my own childhood came flooding back as if it were yesterday. Over the years I had been involved with so much violence that I was determined not to expose my kids to its repercussions, and contrary to my deepest desire to force John to retaliate, I stayed out of it until one Sunday evening, I completely lost control.

On this particular evening the two kids who were John's tormentors stood in front of our house calling out taunts to John, daring him to come out and fight. To make matters worse, these kids were much older than John, and they had turned the kids who were my son's age against him. I was seething. I knew I had to get away from the situation before I exploded. I picked up my car keys and started out to my car so I could cool down by taking a ride to nowhere in particular. As I came out of my house, the kids turned and walked away. I bit my tongue, got into my car, and began to drive off while watching them in the rearview mirror. As I began to pull away from the curb, they turned toward my car and gave me the "finger." That was the 2x4 that broke the camel's back. I jammed the car into reverse and sped toward the kids, who took off running, and luckily for all of us, they had enough of a head start to reach their house before I caught up to them. Now maybe I would have gained control of myself before I reached them, but at the moment I stepped on the gas pedal, my intent was to run them down.

After attempting to live a "normal" life, this incident convinced me that I lacked the courage to risk. I couldn't abide rejection or criticism or failure or any of the other negatives that people encounter, shake off, and go on with their lives. This was the third lifestyle in which I had failed to discover whatever it was I was longing to find. The only difference this time was that the responsibility owed to my family was too great to walk away from, so my coping mechanism was to numb my feelings. The less I felt, the less chance I had of being hurt, and the less I got hurt, the less my anger would erupt. After all, it worked before, why couldn't it work again? My goal now was to provide for the financial needs of my family, to try to guide them, and to keep them from making bad decisions; in other words, to accomplish the duties that the world has assigned to a father and a husband. But I should have been so much more. The time I spent in my room reading and avoiding life should have been spent with them, discovering what they worried about, their likes and dislikes, helping with their homework, and a myriad of things that I avoided because I was too weak and selfish to involve myself with their problems. I should have devoted my life to them; instead I protected myself by adopting a philosophy of "what I didn't know wouldn't hurt me."

Between work and school and homework, there was little time for a social life, which was okay with me. I began to bury myself in my books, much as I had when growing up. The only change was my reading preferences. I now read only nonfiction history, biographies, and memoirs, the exception being any newly released Stephen King book. If a certain subject piqued my interest, I would devour book after book dealing with that topic until I was tired of it. There were stretches of a year or even two years when I would read nothing but American Civil War histories or Hitler biographies[6] or the memoirs and biographies of the musical artists of the sixties, like Dylan or The Doors. They served the same purpose as my reading of the classics: I was able to lose myself in the lives of strangers and relive their successes and failures without

---

[6] I joined the "Book-Of-The-Month Club" in the mid sixties, and the first book I bought was *The Rise and Fall of the Third Reich*, which began a lifelong fascination with Hitler and his henchmen. It boggles the mind how such a group of misfits almost conquered the world.

risking anything of myself. Two years earlier I had witnessed a historical event unfold before my eyes.

November 22, 1963, except for its unusually warm temperature that reached the seventies, began like most workdays. I was working the 2:30 p.m. to 11 p.m. shift in order to pick up an additional 7.5 % shift differential. My schedule was to get up around eleven every morning after staying up until about 3 a.m. watching *The Steve Allen Show* and an old movie. I usually read for an hour and then watched *As the World Turns*, a soap opera that I was hooked on, until one o'clock. Around 12:30 they interrupted the program to report President Kennedy's motorcade had been fired upon. There was then a series of updates culminating with the famous Walter Cronkite announcement of the President's death. I was devastated on so many different levels that I had trouble sorting them out. Kennedy's killing was only the third time a death had invaded my world, the first two being my grandmother and Roger LeClair. JFK's was the first that caused me to break down in tears. When Kennedy ran for President, I wasn't a big fan nor was I politically astute enough to judge his performance as President, but I came to admire him as his term advanced because of his personality and youthful energy. He was such a vital force, especially after the apathy of the Eisenhower years, and to have his life snuffed out in a matter of seconds seemed so senseless, seemed to be such a waste. I cried the entire weekend, and that was the first time I had cried in years and would be the last time I would cry for decades. It was also the first time I felt the heaviness of depression that was to become a familiar companion who would visit with me many times over the ensuing years. The Kennedy assassination reinforced my world view. The world was a broken, painful place that I would do everything in my power to avoid.

The Tet offensive of 1968 was another world event that had a great impact on our family, as it did on so many thousands of others. When we read or discuss history, we need to remember, above all, history is a compendium of thousands upon thousands of individual, personal stories. The war in Viet Nam invaded our family in a very personal way. In February 1968 my parents received a telegram from the Army informing them that my younger brother, Dennis, was seriously wounded, and they would be patching through a telephone call from him as soon as possible. We were very relieved when the call came and we talked to him, because he seemed so upbeat and strong. Our optimism was soon dashed when another telegram came shortly after the first, saying that Dennis had had his leg amputated, in addition to other very serious wounds, and that his life was in grave danger. The government invited my father to come to Japan, where Dennis was in the hospital, because they didn't think he was going to make it. My mother insisted on going with my father, although the government would only pay for one airfare.

My mother came home after a month or two, but my father stayed with my brother until he was able to come home. His permanent losses were an amputated leg, removal of the greater part of his stomach, loss of the use of his left hand (he is left-handed), and a right leg that was severely wounded. When he came home he was sent to Fort Devens, where they had converted some old WWII barracks into a hospital complex. I met the ambulance bus that transported Dennis and other wounded kids from the airport, and I never recognized him as they carried him off the bus on a stretcher. The last time I had seen him, he was over six feet tall and weighed near two hundred pounds, and now he looked like a refugee from a Nazi concentration camp. It was heartbreaking.

THE LONG WAY HOME

Dennis's rehabilitation was a long, hard ordeal. It was also draining on the family, especially for my father. He would make the 140-mile round trip two or three times a week, and after months of this grueling schedule, he began to show the effects of lack of sufficient sleep and the constant worry of the situation. When the time came that the facilities at Devens had little more to offer for Dennis's recovery and he was basically on hold, awaiting a transfer to Valley Forge Rehabilitation Center in Pennsylvania, we requested he be transferred to the naval hospital located in Chelsea, Massachusetts, for the family's sake. If Dennis could be located in Chelsea, as he waited for his transfer, it would reduce our commute by over two-thirds, and it would allow friends and relatives who were unable to get to Devens an opportunity to visit with him and hopefully help raise his spirits.

We immediately ran into a roadblock. We were told a transfer would be impossible, since the Chelsea hospital was a naval facility and Dennis was in the army. That didn't stop my mother. She showed up at Ted Kennedy's office, and although she never got to see him, she left her request with an assistant. Senator Kennedy called back after a couple of weeks and told my mother that, after talking with the doctors at Devens he was convinced Dennis was better off remaining where he was. She then went to the office of the Speaker of the House of Representatives, John McCormack, and made the same request, which eventually led to the same result. Representative McCormack informed her he wouldn't interfere with army rulings, especially medical decisions. Having been turned down by both Kennedy and McCormack, both Irishmen, and one, John McCormack, whose brother and nephew lived in South Boston, my mother was extremely disappointed. Our last chance was Senator Edward

Brooke, the first black man elected to the Senate by popular vote, but if two of our own had refused to help, what were the odds a black man, and a Republican to boot, would buck the system to help a white Irish family originally from South Boston, a town not noted for its liberal voting record (South Boston had voted heavily against Brooke in the last election)? With great trepidation and little confidence in the outcome, she visited the Senator's office, explained why she was there to the secretary, and was asked to wait. Within minutes she was invited into Senator Brooke's office, where she related our problem to him. He asked some questions, took down whatever information he needed to follow up her request, and told my mother he would be in touch. My mother left there thinking that even if this meeting resulted in another dead end, at least the senator had the decency to deal with her on a personal basis and not through secretaries and form letters signed with a stamp.

In a matter of days, Senator Brooke telephoned my mother to inform her that the transfer was scheduled, and Dennis would be in Chelsea very soon. He kept his promise and even went to visit Dennis in the naval hospital once or twice. We will be forever grateful to Senator Brooke not only because he took the time to listen and had the courage to act, but for the lesson we were taught by his actions. Any contention can be reconciled when right- minded people convene to solve a problem, regardless of their differences.

I would be less than honest without touching on the matter of race. South Boston was a racist town, as was every neighborhood in Boston, including the black enclaves. Most of my generation had never met a black, and yet we had an animosity toward them due to the attitudes of our parents and peers. I had left Southie long before the busing problems, but I am of the opinion that had the kids from South Boston been forced to attend schools out of their neighborhoods and were replaced by blond-haired, blue eyed Swedes, the result would have been the same. It was the illogic and unfairness of the decision that united the town, not simply the color of our skins, although race did exacerbate the situation because our outward appearance was so different, it visually defined the conflict.

I became friendly with a black kid when I worked for Gillette. He was the first black person I had any association with, and we really hit it off. We played softball, ate lunch, and had our coffee breaks together. He and I had a lot in common. We read the same books, were sports fans, and shared a similar sense of humor. One day we made plans to go to Suffolk Downs, the local horse track, and on the following Saturday he was to pick me up at my house in South Boston. I worried all week that my friends would see me in a car with a black person, and I would be labeled a "nigger" lover and become alienated from them. I telephoned him on Saturday morning and, to my everlasting shame, made up some lame excuse why I couldn't go to the track with him. I'm sure he knew it was a lie, and our relationship cooled from that point on. I just didn't have the moral courage to do what was right and risk the wrath of my peers. This incident is one more regret of a seemingly endless list of "if onlys."

I pretty much weaned myself from the corner, although there were occasions that took me back to South Boston and the guys. These were the usual events: the weddings, an occasional softball or tag football game, and, unfortunately, a funeral or two. One such time was a bachelor party for someone, I can't recall whom exactly, which took place one Friday night in the late sixties. I was sitting at the bar with Paulie McGonagle and mentioned I couldn't stay long because I had to go into work early the next morning (Saturday) because someone had broken into Gillette and stolen a large amount of razor blades. I was the finished stock analyst, and I needed to inventory the stock to determine what and how much product was missing. Paulie laughed and stated that if I bought him a drink, I wouldn't have to go into work in the morning. When the bartender served Paulie his drink, he reached into his pocket, took out a piece of paper, laughed again, and handed me the paper. It not only was a list of the number of cartons stolen, but it identified the cartons by product code. Instead of working Saturday, I went in an hour early on Monday morning and put my analysis together. In addition to having the weekend off, I was congratulated on the accuracy and timeliness of my report. Somebody should put down on paper all the scams Paulie pulled off in his short lifetime. Everyone has a Paulie story, for good or bad.

The months melted into years, and as the years inevitably advanced, I continued to regress. Whenever I attempted to become more involved in the family, some traumatic event would send me retreating to the sanctuary of my books. Soon after John's problems with the neighborhood kids were solved, we purchased our home in Hanson. I hoped that maybe the move would signal a new beginning; however, it wasn't long before I witnessed Kellie experiencing similar problems with her friends, which caused me to shut down completely.

My daily pattern each morning was to adopt the false persona I had created for myself, which allowed me to survive the workday, arrive home for supper, avoiding any conversation as far as I was able, and retreat to the relative safety of my bedroom. As you might suspect, this behavior didn't exactly endear Peggy to me, and we were losing any sense of intimacy that is so crucial to a successful marriage. On the weekends I usually went into the office on Saturday, ostensibly to catch up on work. In reality, since the place was usually deserted on Saturday, it was another safe place that I could escape to from the pressures I was feeling at home, pressures that emanated from my own personality flaws. Sundays would find me reading the newspapers until early afternoon, when some kind of game would be televised, and I could hide in them for the entire day. My days were spent trying to avoid life as much as humanly possible. A perfect day was one devoid of any emotional pain, and that was accomplished by withdrawing from contact with the outside world that only existed for others. As sad as this seems, I can't remember ever having a good time.

My Achilles heel (an inability to see things through) was beginning to ache. I was in a constant state of anxiety. and bouts of depression were occurring more often at an increasingly exhausting level. When in this state there were days that I had to use all of the will power I could muster just to put my feet on the floor and get out of bed in the morning. I wanted only to curl up into a fetal position and sleep for the rest of my life. Underneath these feelings was a deep aching, a longing for something so much more meaningful and truthful than what this world had to offer. I knew there had to be more, but for me, more was less, and I began to peel layers of my life away with the hope of finding some peace by abandoning the things that I had mastered and no longer had any interest in.

The first to go was school. I had completed about 75% of the required courses for a bachelor's degree in business with an accounting major when I pulled the plug.

I made a couple of half hearted attempts to continue by enrolling in some courses, attending for a few classes, and then dropping out. My college days, or rather nights, were over.

I judiciously used the time that had been dedicated to school for a number of years to self-medicate myself by returning to the solace of alcohol. The Triple O's Bar on Broadway in South Boston was a gathering place for Gillette employees, and I began to spend much too much time there after work. At first it was only on Friday nights, but soon I was there almost every night of the week. I also began an on-again, off-again relationship with a co-worker in Gillette. I suppose I was experiencing what the world calls a mid-life crisis, but it's just another example of the need to have God in our lives and trying to satisfy the longing for Him by filling that special place in us all that is reserved for the Holy Spirit with sex, drugs, alcohol, money, or any other "gods" you may choose. It simply doesn't work.

The next to go was Gillette. I had worked for the company for just a couple of months shy of twenty years, but I walked away without looking back. The time was 1981 and we didn't have the financial needs of prior years because the kids were older and our mortgage and a car payment was about all we owed, so I was able to take a chance and accept a job with the Millipore Corporation, again hoping the change would make a difference in my life. It didn't. My career with Millipore lasted about a year and a half before I resigned. My next try for the brass ring was to found a bookkeeping and tax preparation business. Although it kept us going for a while, I worked out of my house, and not having an office really retarded any potential growth. I then went to work for a guy who sold laser photographs and whose office and warehouse was three minutes from my house. The work was interesting and, even if there wasn't much of a future, I enjoyed it because every day offered something new. One day I would be framing pictures or shipping product or doing the books or delivering and displaying postcards in various retail establishments around the state. After a year or two they moved out of state, and I found myself out of a job, but I always had my bookkeeping and tax preparation skills to fall back on.

And then I committed the ultimate act of quitting. In June of 1985 Peggy and I attended the wedding of one of her co-workers. We were there about an hour, and even though the ceremony and the reception were held out-doors, I suddenly became claustrophobic. The music and the chatter of the wedding guests overwhelmed me, not as sounds, but as if a heavy blanket had been thrown over me, smothering me and not allowing me to breathe. I ran to my car, turned the A/C on full, and drove away. I had never entertained the idea of leaving Peggy and the kids until that moment. As I drove away I was overwhelmed with emotions, feelings of guilt for being selfish, for betraying my family, for being weak and cowardly, but, most of all, for the hurt I was about to inflict on them because I was a failure as a father and as a husband. Peggy didn't deserve this kind of treatment; she was everything a man could hope for—a loving wife and a great mother—and I could not have been prouder of my kids, neither of whom ever gave me any real problems. My rationalization was that I was incapable of having a true relationship with anyone, and I could no longer continue to act out the cha-rade of trying to be someone I wasn't. But regardless of the reason or reasons, once again I had failed to finish, and this time innocent people suffered for it.

CHAPTER 7

BACK TO THE FUTURE

I guess it was inevitable. South Boston has a way of luring its wayward sons home.

When I worked for Gillette, I began to frequent the Triple O's Lounge, located on West Broadway, a two-minute walk from the factory. Over the years, I became friendly with one of the owners, Kevin O'Neil, and we talked about going into business together if the right thing came along. When I moved out of my house in 1984, I rented an apartment in Quincy, which was about a ten-minute ride to Southie and the bar, so I was spending a lot of time there.

About a year before, Whitey Bulger and Kevin Weeks had purchased a package store (a retail liquor store) called Stippo's on Old Colony Avenue. The store couldn't have been in a better location. It was located directly across the street from the Old Colony Housing Project and a half block from the Mary Ellen McCormack (Old Harbor) Housing Project. I was hired as the store's bookkeeper, so I was aware of both its current and potential volume.

On a Wednesday evening, I received a call from Kevin O'Neil asking if I wanted to become a partner with him and purchase the package store. Bulger and Kevin Weeks were asking $300,000 for the business and the inventory, and we would be responsible for the outstanding payables. Being the bookkeeper, I was privy to all the financial data, and it looked like a fair deal. I was out of work and needed to support Peggy and now had the added expense of supporting myself and so I immediately agreed. I met with Kevin the following day (Thursday) and worked out some of the details. Since I was pretty much broke, Kevin agreed to put up some of his property as collateral, and if the deal went through, we would borrow the full amount from a bank. I was at home that evening and thinking about the deal, which I figured might take as long as two to three months for the sale to close, when the phone rang, and my life changed forever.

Kevin O'Neil informed me we were to be at the package store tomorrow (Friday) morning at 8 a.m. because we were the proud new owners. Evidently Whitey Bulger decided he had had enough of the legitimate business world and handed over the keys and the business to Kevin and me with the stipulation we would pursue the financing of the sale with haste. I was yet to realize it, but at 8 a.m. on that fateful Friday, I arrived in the Oceanian state of South Boston and wouldn't return to America for over fifteen years—long after Big Brother had fled.

Thus in less than two days and after less than ten minutes of discussion, we had taken possession of a business that was grossing close to a million dollars without a dime changing hands. This was how Whitey Bulger did business. He didn't require contracts, and he didn't have to deal with the bureaucracy that mere mortals have to endure. He used the ultimate collateral as a guarantee, and that was genuine, knee-buckling fear.

We worked the store from eight in the morning until midnight both Friday and Saturday virtually without a break. And, although I was literally exhausted, the volume of business was mind-boggling. Eventually, we worked out a schedule of hours. Kevin would open the store in the morning, and I reported for work at 2 p.m. and closed at 11 p.m. After closing, there was another hour's work to be done: stocking the beer chests for the next day's sales, reconciling the day's receipts and preparing the deposit. On the way home I would drop the deposit into our bank's night deposit slot. Such was my routine six days a week for the next decade and a half.

I failed to mention my drinking, and I was consuming more than my share. Before going home, after closing the store, I would go to Triple O's most nights until closing time at 2 a.m. and upon arriving home, I would continue to drink until about 4 a.m. when I was, finally, able to sleep. My drink du jour was Absolut vodka with water, and after the first glass I drank it like water.

When we took possession of the package store, we agreed (were instructed) to keep Whitey Bulger, Kevin Weeks, and Stevie Flemmi on the payroll at $500.00 per week for three years. The intent, of course, was to provide a legitimate source of income, but when payday rolled around they endorsed their checks and returned them to me as if they were cashed. They never took any money, and I deposited the checks as part of that day's receipts. In case they weren't available on payday, Whitey provided me with a signature stamp for all three of our "employees."

The irony was they actually did some work on a daily basis. About one-third of our sales were ordered by telephone and delivered by automobiles owned by people we would hire on a daily basis. We paid them a stipend, I think it was $25.00, and they would make pretty good money from tips. The guys would arrive at five o'clock, and Whitey would go straight to the telephone and begin taking the delivery orders. Stevie liked to have the liquor bottles on the shelves stocked in some mysterious method that only he understood. Working alongside Whitey was not very much fun. In truth, it was a downright nerve-racking ordeal. He didn't warm up to new acquaintances easily, and I soon learned not to try to make small talk and kept my mouth shut. As I waited on customers, I could feel Whitey watching and judging me. I breathed a sigh of relief when after a couple of hours he left. This routine went on for months.

I was in for a couple of more surprises. Whitey continued to use the package store to meet people and conduct business. Most of the conversations took place in one of our two beer chests. Due to the insulation needed to keep the beer cold, much to my relief, they were soundproof. I didn't want to overhear anything because like Sgt. Schultz I didn't want to "know nothing." Soon, I realized this was serious, about as serious as it can get, and I had to be "on my toes" constantly. One wrong word, no matter how innocently intended, had the potential to alter how I was perceived and perception was reality to Whitey.

Another frequent occurrence was Kevin Weeks knocking someone unconscious, either in the parking lot, or in one of the beer chests. Kevin was the toughest kid and hardest puncher I had ever personally observed. Usually the confrontations in the beer chest were the enforcement of some rules the guilty party had broken. He would be contacted and told to meet Kevin at the package store, and when he arrived at the arranged time, Kevin and he would go into the beer chest. I would hear a muffled crash and in a few minutes Kevin's guest would stagger out of the chest usually trying to stem the bleeding by holding a handkerchief to a particular region of his face.

Every so often, someone would open the door to the package store, poke his head in, and offer an invite to Kevin to come outside to continue a fight they had the night before. Kevin would go out to our parking lot, throw a punch or two, and knock the person out. He would then come back into the store and continue our conversation as if nothing had occurred. I would discover later that Kevin had knocked him out the night before, and yet the kid came after him the next day and was knocked out again. I could never see the logic, and yet this scene was repeated again and again. Why did they think the results would be any different the second time? The only answer I'm able to come up with is this was South Boston.

Shortly after we purchased the store, we renamed it The South Boston Liquor Mart and had a large shamrock painted on one of the exterior walls. This turned out to be not such a great idea. The shamrock became the equivalent to a sound bite for the press and the television media. From the moment the shamrock was displayed, it, and consequently the building, became the backdrop for any Whitey Bulger breaking news stories, and in later years, there were plenty. I am still asked, twenty years later, if I owned the store with the shamrock.

Business was brisk. We didn't have any problem borrowing the $300,000 purchase price for the business based on the store's sales and the property Kevin O'Neil was able to pledge as collateral. Contrary to the belief of everyone from the man in the street to the media and law enforcement, Whitey never took a penny out of the business, other than the original purchase price, nor was he

ever a silent partner. We owned it lock, stock, and barrel.
Our sales peaked in 1987 at two million, two hundred
thousand dollars. The drug of choice during the mid to
late eighties was cocaine, and I always had a theory that
cocaine and alcohol went hand in hand. The more cocaine
that the neighborhood snorted, the more alcohol they
consumed. Also, there was a lot of money on the street,
and it wasn't being earned on nine-to-five jobs. The most
common sources of income were dealing cocaine,
shoplifting, tailgating (stealing goods from the back of
trucks), and the more violent crimes of jewelry store rob-
beries and an occasional armored car hold up. I was always
aware when someone made a score because they would
purchase cases of Dom Perignon or Cristal champagne at
about $120 a bottle. This didn't strike me as an average
purchase for an unemployed 21-year-old.

Almost from the beginning, I knew this endeavor
would end badly. Ever since I can remember, I needed to
be entirely independent, to be my own man. I detested
having to bend my will to anyone, and now I had to be
careful of what I said and did. I was a prisoner to the business six days a week, and on Sunday, I spent the day in bed
recovering from the quantity of alcohol I had consumed
Saturday night and Sunday morning. My partner's view of
me was that I was an employee and he was the owner. He
made the decisions and I was informed only after the fact.
The situation was untenable, but I was locked in financially. I had moved in with a girl whom I had known years
earlier from Gillette and who would later become my wife,
and in addition to my financial responsibility to Peggy, and
trying to help with Joan's rent, I couldn't afford to miss a
paycheck, never mind be out of work for any extended
period of time. Once again I was forced to remain in a job
that I loathed because I had to make a buck.

My sense of impending trouble, however, originated from other sources. The first event that made me uneasy occurred when the Internal Revenue Service called to inform me they were auditing Stippo's Liquor Store's 1984 tax return, which I had prepared. An IRS. supervisor and auditor visited the liquor store and wanted to see the cash register tapes for 1984, which I provided. They said they would return to total the tapes and compare the amount on the tapes to the sales reported on the tax return, but first they wanted to meet with me at their office to discuss the return.

I met with the auditor and became perplexed with his questions, most of which had nothing to do with the return. His queries were aimed at how many hours Whitey, Stevie, and Kevin were present at the store and if they invested their own money to purchase it. My answer to most of his questions was I didn't know because I didn't. He excused himself and came back with the supervisor who had visited the store. They discussed something among themselves and then the supervisor told me they might have a criminal case here and set a date for me to come back with the year-end inventory records.

When I arrived home, the first thing I did was contact a lawyer, and after relating the events of the day, his recommendation was that he should accompany me to the next scheduled meeting. On the designated day, as we met with the supervisor and auditor, my lawyer informed them he was there because during the previous meeting, criminal activity was mentioned. The supervisor denied ever saying anything about criminal activity and immediately left us alone with the auditor. He asked one question concerning the inventory records, made a copy of them, and adjourned the meeting. Six weeks later I received a letter from the IRS. stating that the audit had been completed and there wouldn't be any change. This was my initiation to the tactics used by law enforcement when they were seeking information. The future would hold more such confrontations.

In January 1987 our local PBS station, Channel 2, ran an investigative program reporting the ties between Whitey Bulger and our liquor store. The program alleged our purchase of the store was a sham meant to hide Bulger's interest in the business. The airing of the program was worrisome for a couple of reasons. One was the embarrassment it caused my family, especially since it wasn't true, and another element of the investigative report that worried me was my sense the story was given to PBS by law enforcement or, at least, aired with their blessing. I took this as a clear indication the law was beginning to turn up the pressure on Whitey Bulger. My apprehension arose from knowing my name was out there now. It was on all the legal documents pertaining to the store, it was known to the IRS. because of my involvement as Whitey's bookkeeper, and whenever the press ran a story on him, they managed to mention me and the liquor store somewhere in the text. As if that wasn't enough, I was now preparing Bulger's personal income tax returns. If I wasn't already, it would only be a matter of time before I became a person of interest to the powers that be.

My intuition that the law enforcement agencies were becoming more active was born out in March of 1989 when the Boston police detained one of our delivery kids as he was delivering a carload of beer to a private club. Evidently it is illegal for a retail liquor store to sell alcohol to any establishment to be resold. We had a number of bars and private clubs who purchased beer from the Liquor Mart on a weekly basis. We sold it to them for one reason, and that was to increase our sales, but when the detective's affidavit was released to the press, it stated that Bulger and his associates were operating a Prohibition-era conspiracy by distributing liquor to circumvent state tax and alcohol laws. The affidavit went on to say that Bulger was hiding his financial interest in the liquor business. The other interesting piece of information revealed that Bulger and the liquor store had been under intense surveillance for at least a year.

I never understood how any sales tax was avoided, and once again it was asserted Bulger had a hidden interest in the liquor store. After all the dust settled, we were told to desist from delivering beer to other liquor establishments and the matter was closed.

Another incident that foreboded future problems occurred in December 1989 when I was introduced to F.B.I. Special Agent John Connolly. John had a list of alcohol he wished to purchase for the bureau's Boston office Christmas party. The warning bells in my mind went off like a three-alarm fire. Why in the world would an F.B.I. agent purchase a large quantity of liquor from a package store that was reputed to be a gang headquarters and ostensibly owned by the most infamous criminal in Boston? I hadn't any answer, and I knew enough not to ask the question.

My anxiety level was consistently high. To use a current description, I was self-medicating, and my drug of choice was alcohol. I never drank during the day but once I left work I threw down drink after drink until the world went away. Brick in Tennessee Williams' book, *Cat on a Hot Tin Roof*, uttered the best description of this process I ever heard when he said he drank until he heard that "click in his head that made him feel peaceful." Things weren't progressing exactly how I had hoped. I hated my job and I knew it was only a matter of time before the law would focus their attention on me. I was the poster boy for the quasi-honest person who law enforcement thought would cooperate if they found some punishable offense they might use as a lever, a bargaining chip. The only uncertainty was what form the threat would take. In the meantime, I didn't understand how Whitey and Kevin Weeks held to the same routine and seemed to be in the same place at the same time day after day. Was I the only one who noticed the heightened police activity or was it simply my imagination? Maybe the street smarts I had developed years ago on the corner of O and 2nd streets had deserted me and been replaced with paranoia.

For a couple of years, Kevin O'Neil and I had been lobbying Kevin Weeks to sell the building that housed the package store to us. We had been paying $1,500 ($500 each) a month rent to Whitey, Kevin Weeks, and Mary Flemmi, who was Stevie Flemmi's mother. One afternoon in December 1989, one of the players, I can't recall who, said to meet Whitey at a lawyer's office in the morning to pass papers on the building. I screwed up the courage to ask the amount of the selling price and, almost reluctant to hear the answer, was told it was $400,000, which I thought was quite fair.

We met the next morning, signed the necessary papers, and were finished in about fifteen minutes. This manner of doing business was classic Whitey Bulger. There wasn't any negotiation, any appraisal, any closing papers or, for that matter, a down payment. The sole process that in any way resembled a bureaucratic event was signing our names on the appropriate lines.

The purchase of the building lifted my spirits. It represented the light at the end of the tunnel. South Boston was beginning to show signs of a real estate boom with condominiums springing up all over the city that were being purchased by young professionals who worked in downtown Boston, which was only a fifteen-minute bus ride away. We now had a couple of alternatives. We could continue to grow the business and eventually sell the liquor store and the building, or we could develop the land into a high- rise condominium. Our building was directly across from Marine Park, a grassy expanse of land containing playing fields, and just beyond the park was the ocean. The parcel of land on which our liquor store sat could be a very desirable and therefore profitable piece of land.

My elation lasted for about three weeks. In early January 1990, the newspapers reported that Whitey Bulger netted $360,000 in a one-day Southie property sale. Evidently Whitey had purchased the building from Kevin Weeks and Mary Flemmi for $40,000 on the same morning we bought it from him for $400,000. Once again my name was part of the news item, and once again it was linked to Whitey Bulger. I didn't care for myself; I had long since ceased fretting about what others may think of me, but once again, my family would be embarrassed, and once again, it reinforced the law's suspicion that I was a straw acting as a front man for Bulger, increasing the chance I would be targeted in some manner. I knew Whitey to be a very intelligent individual, and I wondered why he seemed to carry out his schemes in such a public manner. If I were a member of the organized crime unit, I would take Bulger's machinations very personally and redouble my efforts to nail him. I thought at the time he was merely arrogant, but in retrospect I see why he could afford to flaunt his exploits. He had someone watching his back.

As the years went by, Whitey warmed up to me. And, although I would never initiate the conversation, if he wanted to talk, I listened, hoping he wouldn't say anything I didn't want to hear. Sometimes he did, which I mention in an ensuing chapter. Two such conversations come to mind, and if it were anyone but James "Whitey" Bulger speaking, I would have dismissed them as bravado.

He told me one night that he would never allow himself to be arrested because he didn't intend to give the arresting officers the satisfaction of pasting into their scrapbooks newspaper photographs of him being escorted in handcuffs into some police station. I remember the other monologue (conversations with him consisted mainly of listening) because Whitey was in a rare reflective mood. I only witnessed him in this frame of mind two or three times. It was as if he dropped the need to be on guard and was able to shed, if only for a few moments, his social awkwardness, so obvious to anyone who paid the least attention. I thought maybe I was wrong about him, and his tough guy act was just that, an act made necessary by his "business." My presumption of Whitey's hidden humanitarian nature was soon dashed upon the rocks of reality as his small talk took a dramatic turn and he began to speak of death. He told me that if he were diagnosed with terminal cancer or any fatal disease, he had a "hit" list of enemies whom he intended to kill before he passed away. I never again searched for Whitey's more gentle nature.

I knew I had gained Whitey's trust when I was included on his Christmas list. He knew I was an animal lover and owned a cat that I loved, so on consecutive Christmases he gave me a very expensive Lalique cat and, on another, a Movado watch. Actually, he would ask Kevin Weeks to give out the presents, maybe because he felt embarrassed at being a nice guy. Christmas wasn't the only time he would give me a gift. At various times, and for no apparent reason, Whitey gave me a great full-length winter coat, a pair of cuff links with $2.50 gold centerpieces, and more fitting to his personality, a garrison belt with a buckle that could be unsnapped from the belt and when removed, became a short, dangerous-looking knife. Whitey also gave me a number of stiletto type folding knives along with a tutorial on how to use them. He cautioned me to be especially careful when stabbing an individual because upon impact my hand may slide down the blade, thus inflicting a serious injury on my palm or fingers or both.

Word spreads quickly in South Boston. So it didn't take long for the town to assume I was with "Whitey," whatever that meant. I think it meant to Whitey and Kevin Weeks that they would take any disrespect aimed at me as a personal insult to them. This paternalism didn't necessarily have anything to do with me; it had everything to do with not allowing any act that may be construed as subversive to go unpunished. It was absolutely vital that anything that even suggested a threat to Bulger's autonomy and respect be immediately squelched.

Having sampled a small taste of unmerited respect and special treatment bestowed on me by the town simply because I was perceived to be with "Whitey," I understood the allure of being a "wise guy." There isn't a better feeling than walking into a bar and, as the theme song from the television sitcom Cheers recounts, "everyone knows your name." My personality demanded I keep a low profile yet I found it almost impossible not to be flattered when I entered a store or a bar or anywhere people were gathered, and noticed they would, in hushed voices, inform each other who I was or, more to the point, who they conceived I was. Girls wanted to be seen with me, and I couldn't possibly drink all the glasses of vodka and water sent over to my table, sometimes by people I didn't know, or at least didn't recall. And I experienced only a fraction of the fringe benefits the genuine "wise guys" routinely received.

One night I sampled how the power and fear assigned to Whitey, Stevie, and Kevin can cause a potentially bad situation to just go away. A friend and I had gone out to eat at Amrheins, a local restaurant, and on the way, we stopped into Triple O's for a couple of drinks. The place was empty, except for one guy sitting half-way down the bar. I knew him to be trouble. When he had a few drinks, he liked to instigate a fight with anyone available. The old-timers used to say of a person who got nasty when he drank that his alcohol was poured from a Jack Dempsey bottle. Anyway, we were there for only a couple of minutes when he began to heckle us. I walked up to him and told him to keep his mouth shut, and much to my surprise he got up from the bar stool and walked out the door. The bartender told us this was the only time she had ever seen him walk away from a fight. Later, he told a friend of mine how he almost picked a fight with a guy, until he realized it was Stevie Flemmi. The incident ended almost before it began because I was mistaken for Stevie and because of the fear exercised by him and his partners.

On consecutive days in early August 1990, a task force consisting of officers from the Drug Enforcement Administration (DEA), the Bureau of Alcohol, Tobacco and Firearms (ATF), the Internal Revenue Service (IRS) and the Boston Police arrested fifty-one people on drug trafficking charges. The arrests were a culmination of a concerted three-year investigation by the above-mentioned task force. Our liquor store was, of course, one of the homes and businesses entered and searched, and although no one was arrested, they seized a number of records and actually confiscated a number of bottles of beer that were tested for authenticity. I don't know if this was standard operating procedure or the ATF actually suspected us of brewing or diluting our beer.

Beyond the obvious consequences of the adverse publicity and the effect it had on my family, this time was even more demeaning because my name was now linked to drug trafficking. The first thing that struck me was that the F.B.I. was not included as part of the task force. In 1988, *The Boston Globe* ran a four-part *Spotlight Report* on the Bulger brothers. They theorized that Whitey was an F.B.I. informant, and John Connolly was likely to be his handler. It didn't take a genius to consider the exclusion of the F.B.I. in the drug crackdown, the *Globe* Spotlight series, and Connolly's purchase of liquor from our store to determine that one and one and one equals three.

It was at this moment, I was sure my premonition of impending doom was inevitable. I felt events were going downhill and were beginning to accelerate out of control. This latest police action just about convinced me Whitey was both an informant and that he had his hands in the drug business. I felt betrayed and foolish, for I had vehemently defended him on these two issues to anyone who would listen. I had been present on many occasions as he ranted against the "rats" and the "druggies" and their pushers, and I bought into his apparent sincerity lock, stock, and barrel. Yet I may have been mistaken. After all, Whitey wasn't arrested, and he didn't seem worried by any of the police activity or the ensuing publicity. I couldn't decide if Bulger was a hypocrite and a liar or the victim of a police/media smear campaign to turn public opinion and organized crime against him. He would have a tough time doing business in a city that thought him an informer. In fact, he'd have a tough time staying alive. I just didn't know.

One lesson learned was once law enforcement believed something to be true, it was next to impossible for them to change their minds. In the days following the raid, the media quoted police sources as to Whitey having a hidden interest in the liquor store and that the sale of the building was a sham sale, and Whitey was the de facto owner; both of which were untrue. They rehashed the illegal liquor deliveries and characterized them as a Bulger conspiracy to avoid sales and income taxes about which they promised to convene a grand jury to investigate the charges. Once again, the only motive for these deliveries was to increase our sales. And furthermore, the only taxes due on the sale of alcohol in those days were included in the purchase price from the wholesaler, and we paid those when we bought the beer. As for the income tax avoidance, we included these deliveries in our sales numbers. We actually rang them up on our cash register. Now I don't deny what we did was illegal, but it was a misdemeanor at best, and should have been and was addressed by the liquor licensing board. We were told to cease the deliveries. We complied and the matter was dropped. Another erroneous supposition was a small plastic box with the word "cuff" written on it. It contained thirty or forty names and addresses written on index cards. When the police came across this box during the search of the liquor store, they informed the press that the word "cuff" was a bookmaker's term for money owed to them by bettors. That may be true, I don't know, but I do know the merchants in the neighborhood, to keep track of the goods they sold on credit, use it a lot more frequently. There wasn't any bookmaking activity that took place at the liquor store.

Ironically, the one incriminating document seized during the raid wasn't even illegal. Much to the glee of the task force, they discovered the receipt for the alcohol sold to the F.B.I. as door prizes for their Christmas party. This proven connection between the liquor store and the F.B.I. justified the exclusion of the Bureau from the task force. They not only had not invited the F.B.I. to participate, but went to great pains to hide the planned offensive from them. The task force was ecstatic.

The liquor store was the visual icon for any press or television story on the raid or on any Bulger story for that matter. I recall watching a five o'clock newscast whose lead story, of course, was the arrests, and as the newsman reported, that guns, money, and drugs were seized during the raid. The video on the television screen showed detectives coming out of our store carrying bags of innocuous records but giving the impression to anyone watching the broadcast they were carrying out guns and drugs. I saw my dream of selling the business and the building disintegrate as the newscaster broke to commercial.

It seemed as if I was the only one who was concerned. I saw the events of the last couple of years as not only a continuation, but an escalation by law enforcement to nail Bulger, but the players casually went about their business as usual. In the end everyone was partially right. Whitey was finally indicted but not for five more eventful years.

The best was yet to come. On a late July afternoon in 1991, two representatives of the Massachusetts Lottery Commission visited the liquor store and informed me that we had sold a $14,328,960 winning lottery ticket. After refusing to have my picture taken, I asked the representative if he knew the winner's name. His answer was Michael Linskey. Mike was Patty Linskey's brother, who was a friend and who worked in the liquor store with us. Wow, I thought. We will receive a $25,000 commission for selling the ticket, and I was sure Mike would share the winnings with Patty. We were all winners. Little did I know just how many.

Patty's son and I drove to Patty's house to inform him of the hit, and after he called his brother to confirm it, we all went barhopping to celebrate Patty's good fortune. Somewhere along the line we hooked up with Kevin Weeks and I don't recall who else and wound up the night at Triple O's until closing time at 2 a.m. The other shoe wouldn't drop for two or three more days.

I awoke on Tuesday, July 30, 1991 to a headline in *The Boston Globe* that made my stomach flip. It read, "Whitey Bulger shares $14M lottery prize." Evidently, Mike and Patty Linskey were partners in the winning ticket, and Patty, Kevin Weeks, and Whitey Bulger split Patty's share. Once again I couldn't understand why Whitey would rub the law's nose in the dirt and make his arrest a personal thing. Maybe it was essential for him to have a legitimate income of $89,000 a year for twenty years, but there must have been a way to accomplish that end in a much less public way. I don't know, I certainly wasn't privy to his thoughts, but I knew the moment I saw that headline, nothing good would come from it. The media attention heightened, and that same old stock photograph of the store and its ill-advised shamrock was again plastered over the newspapers and was the backdrop during the television newscasts of the event.

The initial hue and cry from the media was that Bulger had somehow rigged the lottery. As further proof, the ticket was purchased in a "mob-controlled liquor store," and Whitey's store at that. Although there was not one iota of illegality, the media forced the poor lottery officials to jump through hoops. They were forced to try and prove a negative and so the lottery turned to the liquor store. First they discovered Kevin Weeks' name was still listed as the lottery sales agent even though he had sold the business to Kevin O'Neil and me in 1986 and used this technicality to not award the liquor store the $25,000 commission (it was later found that the lottery had received the transfer notification but had not recorded it). We obtained a lawyer and the commission was paid within a week or two. Law enforcement was shocked and angry. I could feel the emotion from the interviewed officers jump off the printed page.

I was present when the eventual winning ticket was sold. In December 1991, Patty Linskey bought ten Mass Millions season tickets as Christmas presents, one of which he gave to his brother Mike. In fact, I received one of the ten tickets. I haven't any knowledge what agreements were in place, and it really doesn't matter because the only act that could be construed as illegal would be if they coerced Mike to share the ticket, and I know that wasn't the case. I can't imagine the uproar if I was presented with the winning ticket. The headlines would have read "Straw for Whitey hits lottery with a ticket sold in mob-controlled store." Bulger's lottery windfall added another chapter to his legend and further proof of his invincibility.

One of the perks of having a store that everyone believed to be owned by Whitey Bulger was safety. Anyone who even heard of him knew better than to cause any problem in the store or, God forbid, rob the place. The threat now came in the person of strangers from outside of South Boston. In 1990, the city of Boston began a two-year plan to integrate public housing, and by 1993 they had pretty much accomplished their goals. The inhabitants of the housing projects were not the problem; it was the younger people who came into Southie from other parts of the city to visit friends and relatives. These guys didn't know of Whitey's reputation and I don't think the two I became acquainted with one night in the fall of 1993 would have cared anyway.

It was about 9:00 one Friday or Saturday evening when two black kids who looked to be in their early twenties came into the store. The moment I saw them, my stomach filled with butterflies, and the adrenaline began its familiar rush through my body. I've always had the ability to anticipate potential trouble, and unless I had suddenly become paranoid, these guys were trouble with a capital T. One of them slowly walked the length of the store, while the second kid remained by the door. On his way back to the front of the store, he stopped and asked me the price of a bottle of champagne. He told me the price was too high, and they both left the store. I knew I hadn't seen the last of them. This was the only time I wished we had a pistol in the store, something I never wanted because of the potential it might be used for the wrong reason.

After about ten minutes, my two friends paid us another visit and repeated their performance of one staying at the door and the other walking to the rear of the store. This time I was trying to come up with some sort of defensive action. I had a baseball bat and a knife, but I was sure these guys were armed with guns and I would never get close enough to use either. My coworker was a girl, so not only couldn't I expect any help from that end, but I had to try and keep her out of harm's way. I felt the only thing stopping them from making their move was the night of the week. It was a weekend and there was a steady flow of customers in and out of the store.

As the guy who had walked to the rear of the store started back up towards the door he complimented me on how well stocked the store was and remarked how I must do a good business. Now it was really getting dangerous because we had looked into each other's eyes when he was talking to me, and if they robbed me now, they would have to shoot me. When the two of them left for the second time, I began to telephone people who might be in the area and could quickly get to the store. But to no avail, I couldn't contact anyone. When they came in for the third time, I was thinking about going on the offense and taking out the "stroller" with the baseball bat, but that still left the other guy too far away to reach before he could pull his gun. God was with us that night because it was one of the busiest nights we had in a long time, and the store never had fewer than five or six people shopping at any one time. They left and never came back.

The reason they never came back was, a few days later, they were arrested for shooting and killing an off-duty police officer on a private security detail while he slept in his car. I recognized their pictures in the newspaper, and I thanked God for His intervention that night. The reader may ask why I didn't call the police. My answer is it never crossed my mind. I was from Southie.

Just prior to the above-mentioned incident, we received more unwanted publicity. The *Boston Herald* reported that a lien had been filed against the liquor store by the Massachusetts Department of Revenue for back corporate and sales taxes amounting to $12,526. All of which was true, but what they failed to mention was we had entered into a payment plan with the state, and by the time the article ran in the newspaper, the taxes were all but paid.

What bothered me most was how the story was handled. Of course the ubiquitous picture of the liquor store accompanied the article, and they had to include that Bulger used the store to control the wholesale liquor trade in

South Boston, and it was the site of the infamous lottery ticket sale that netted Bulger a share of a $14.3 million Mass Millions jackpot. And to top it off, they reported in the same story of a lien of $95,048 against a café where Mafia boss Jerry Angiulo frequented. Now we were mentioned in the same breath as the Mafia. Things were going splendidly.

I admit I hated the media and for good reason. They were fortunate if half of their stories' content was factual, at least those written about the liquor store. I never held any bad feelings about law enforcement except for their penchant for coming to an erroneous conclusion and never letting go of it. But I understood their position and the way Whitey seemed to flaunt his exploits; if I were in their shoes, I would have done anything to get him. My problem was, maybe for the first time in my life, I was really naïve. I thought I would be able to purchase the store, keep my nose clean, and I would be left alone. I actually believed that I couldn't be found guilty by association. I was beginning to shed that notion.

CHAPTER 8

THE OTHER GUY

*J*ames "Whitey" Bulger was the ultimate control freak. There wasn't anything too small or too trivial to escape his attention. He would lecture us on the kind of food to eat or not to eat and caution us against the danger of tobacco, alcohol, and drugs. He would buy the *Boston Herald* newspaper every day (he considered *The Boston Globe* a personal enemy) and bring it back the following day so I could return it to the *Boston Herald* delivery person for credit. Our liquor store was longer than it was wide, and the six-pack chests were located at the far end of the store. Whitey suggested whenever I had occasion to go to the rear of the store that I complete at least three tasks, thus limiting the number of trips back and forth from the front. He estimated it would save tens of thousands of steps in a year. When Whitey noticed I was suffering from acid reflux disease and was eating Rolaids like candy, he touted me on to the other brand so I might benefit from the added calcium in Tums. On a particularly cold day, he noticed I wore a leather coat. Whitey commented that although leather looked good, it wasn't very warm, I agreed and immediately forgot about the conversation. Two weeks later Kevin

Weeks (Whitey seldom handed out a gift in person) presented me with a down-filled, three-quarter-length winter coat that Whitey purchased from The Company Store, a mail order outfit, because the coat I was wearing wouldn't keep me warm enough. Whitey gave so many of these coats to so many people, they took on the look of a uniform.

I don't think Bulger ever did anything without a motive, and benevolent or not, his suggestions were not suggestions, they were directives. He felt anyone who was connected to his world reflected on him and so had to pass muster in attitude, appearance, and action. Kevin O'Neil, my partner, informed me one day, "the other guy"[7] wanted me to remove my wedding ring because a ring implied the wearer was "hen-pecked." I stopped wearing my wedding ring just as I had switched to Tums and wore my Company Store coat.

I should note, I was fiercely independent and passionately resented anyone trying to control my actions or my thoughts. But I swallowed hard and went along with a smile, because, having recently separated from my wife, I had some heavy financial responsibilities and I had a dream. My hope was to grow the business, buy the building, and in four or five years sell both and get out of there with enough capital to plan the rest of my life. If I tried to be my own man, in Whitey's world, none of this would be possible. I had to keep a low profile and survive the next few years if my dream had any chance of coming to fruition.

---

[7] "The other guy" was a code name for Whitey Bulger primarily used when talking on a phone or in a location that may have electronic surveillance or when strangers were in earshot, although by this time, law enforcement had long since broken the code and were well aware of the identity of "the other guy."

To give the devil his due, and contrary to everyone's belief, notably law enforcement and the media, Bulger never took a penny from the business except the agreed-upon purchase price. In fact, he always paid for anything he took, whether it be an occasional bottle of wine or the daily newspaper. That's not to say that Whitey Bulger didn't control everyone and everything that remotely fell into his sphere of influence—he did.

I am always amused when well-meaning people inform me in no uncertain terms that they would never allow anyone like Whitey Bulger to control their lives. This attitude is both logical and instinctual but extremely dangerous. My response is always the same. If your intent is to stand up to people like Whitey, then be prepared to be, at best, hurt very badly and at worst, killed. These are the consequences for matters as trivial as demonstrating a little disrespect. If you are not prepared to kill a person like Whitey Bulger, then I suggest you either go along or go away and go as far and as fast as possible. I find the media and those inhabitants of suburbia who encourage inner-city dwellers to report criminal activity to the police and to testify against the felons so naïve as to be almost criminal. I think it very disingenuous for those out of harm's way to ask others to act in a manner that may end in their death or intimidation or worse to their families. The witness protection program was devised for this purpose. These guys don't fool around, and their threats are promises. The world of Whitey Bulger and of the people like him has its own laws; they are the legislators, the Supreme Court and they run the penal system.

Being around Whitey was like walking a tightrope without a net, and one wrong word or the hint of a subversive attitude could set the wire to swaying. One night I thought I lost my footing. Whitey came into the store around eight or nine one evening and said he wanted to talk to me. We went to the rear of the store, where Whitey asked if I would like to make five thousand dollars. I was trying very hard to get involved in as little criminal activity as possible, and although I didn't yet know what Whitey had in mind, I knew I wasn't interested. In return for the money, he wanted me to supply the Irish Republican Army with my driver's license and social security card. Although he never talked about the details, I assumed my credentials would aid in obtaining armaments. These weapons would likely be used by the IRA against the British and/or Northern Ireland, and the last thing I wanted on my conscience was to be complicit in the death of another human being. I steeled myself to look him in the eyes, and fearing to utter the "no" word, a word Bulger rarely accepted graciously, I asked, lamely, for some time to think it over. His entire countenance changed, and his eyes flashed with anger as he turned away and without a word stormed out of the store. Whitey stopped coming into the Liquor Mart, and as each passing day added to his absence, my apprehension heightened, and I began to look over my shoulder when closing the store at night and glanced, frequently, into the rearview mirror on my drive home. After two or three weeks, Whitey walked into the store as if nothing had happened. Maybe nothing had happened as far as he was concerned, but I know it was the only time in my life I was elated to see Whitey Bulger.

Whitey was a man of contradictions. I guess what set him apart was he was rarely contradicted. He never ceased to amaze me, and just when I thought I had him figured out, he would do something completely out of character. There were nights, at closing time, I would see Whitey's car parked far up the block, and as an occasional passing car's headlights illuminated the interior of his automobile,

I would catch a glimpse of him watching me through a pair of binoculars, as I counted out the day's receipts. I can only think he was spying on me to see if I was skimming cash from my partner, and then, soon after attempting to prove me a thief, he gave me seven thousand dollars to cover a series of uninsured medical procedures required to eliminate some growths in my neck. Kevin Weeks, who informed Whitey of my problem, handed me the money and told me it was a gift and was not to be repaid. Whitey never once mentioned it to me.

He hated blacks but didn't allow any disparaging remarks pointed at Italians. I recall Kevin O'Connor, a friend of mine, telling me a joke whose punch line contained the word "Guinea." Later that same night I was talking to Whitey when Kevin joined us, and I thought Oh no! Kevin is going to tell that joke to Whitey, and sure enough, Kevin asked Whitey if he had heard the one about the Irishman and the Italian. I tried to head him off by nudging him in the side with a discreet elbow, but Kevin ignored the hint and continued with the joke. I quickly excused myself and headed to the rear of the store, where I wouldn't have to witness Whitey's reaction to the punch line. Kevin soon joined me, looking a bit shaken, and informed me he didn't think Whitey thought the joke very funny because he gave Kevin an angry look and walked away. I suggested that Kevin may want to substitute a Russian or an Englishman for the Italian next time. I guess you might say Whitey was bigoted, politically correct, and a multiple killer. Tony Soprano could have been modeled on him.

Whitey was a masterful manipulator, and observing him wield his power was both fascinating and frightening. Intimidation was always the quickest and easiest method of controlling a situation, and his reputation for violence was usually enough to achieve his ends. It was important, therefore, to maintain that reputation, so when actual violence was required—a physical beating, or worse—it became public knowledge so as to reinforce the fear factor. Once someone was aware of what Whitey was capable of, he would need only slight prodding to fall in line. For example, I had recently been subpoenaed to appear before a grand jury convened to look at the Bulger organization. One morning Bulger, Kevin Weeks, and I were standing around talking about nothing in particular, Kevin stated to Whitey that "Fitzy" Fitzpatrick, a kid who worked for Kevin O'Neil at the Triple O's bar, was subpoenaed for the same grand jury that very day. Whitey, looking at me intently, replied to Kevin, "Let's kill him." Now I have no doubt this whole charade was meant to send me a message which I received loud and clear, and they had never entertained the idea of killing "Fitzy."

I am a student of history, and I remember, at the time, thinking the only difference between the raw power wielded by Bulger and that of a Hitler or a Stalin or a Mao is the scale and scope of that power. The methods are identical. A larger- than-life leader exercises pure power by generating a fear of punishment in those whom he wishes to control, while insisting on conformity of thought and action, instilling in them a chauvinistic belief in their society, and depending on the existence of an intelligence network.

Whitey created and increased the fear factor with every act of enforcement and was masterful in its use, while he never wavered in the indoctrination of his version of a moral code, the foundation of which was keeping one's mouth shut. He gathered information in a couple of ways. Like all men of power, people wanted to endear themselves to him, and they attempted to accomplish this by whispering in his ear. The information they supplied ran the gamut from who may have taken down an armored car to letting him know who was bad-mouthing him. Another source, as we now know, was the Federal Bureau of Investigation; their motives for collaborating are a little more complex. But the real genius of Bulger was in appropriating the values of the town to further his own ends. South Boston people thought the town a very special place and were sensitive to any criticism and extremely protective of their own. Whitey never missed an opportunity to demonstrate he was one of their own.

Mussolini was said to make "the trains run on time," and Whitey Bulger, too, contributed a certain order to the town. He closed down crack houses that were beginning to spring up; he intervened in neighborhood feuds. He put a stop to kids who were terrorizing the weak and the elderly. He was able to accomplish these ends because raw power made him a law unto himself. If an elderly lady was being harassed by a neighbor or a group of teenagers, she needn't struggle through the bureaucracy of the legal system by reporting the problem to the police and then appearing before a judge to have a restraining order issued, which would immediately be ignored and would, in fact, escalate the situation. She need only get the word to Whitey and the problem would go away. If a group of addicts confiscated an abandoned building and turned it into a crack house, the police would roust them and they'd be back within hours, but when Whitey was involved, they moved out permanently, sometimes with just a word and sometimes with a bit more force. There was one addict who was breaking into homes to support his habit, and after taking a beating, Whitey exiled him from South Boston. He never came back. I've witnessed elderly ladies thanking him with tears in their eyes for warning away

their tormentors or for sending them an order of groceries; mothers and fathers telling him how a child who
was beginning to use drugs straightened out after Whitey
had a talk with him; middle-aged men and women thank-
ful for his help with a legal problem, and the stories go on
and on.

The reverse of the coin is that Bulger very seldom did
anything without an ulterior motive, and the by-product
of his benevolent deeds was goodwill. He had a Robin
Hood-like reputation in the town, and when less than flat-
tering stories were reported by the media, the town stood
behind him almost to a man. When *The Boston Globe* ini-
tially broke the story of Whitey's informant status with the
F.B.I., the townies, me included, scoffed at the very idea
and defended him with great passion. It was unthinkable
that this man who hated "rats" and preached against
"squealing," who did his time in Alcatraz like a man and
stood up in the shooting war with the Mullens, who loved
"Southie" and helped to keep its neighborhoods crime-
free, could be an informer. It was thought to be just
another example of the *Globe's* vendetta against the Bulger
brothers specifically and South Boston in general. Simi-
larly in August 1990, fifty-one people were indicted on
drug charges and arrested in a sweeping drug raid conducted by the Drug Enforcement Agency, the Department of Alcohol, Tobacco, and Firearms, and the local and
state police. The media reported those arrested as members of the Bulger organization, and once again, the town
rallied around Whitey because they knew how he hated
drugs. After all, didn't he close down the crack houses and
kick the street pushers out of "Southie," and didn't he
warn against using alcohol let alone drugs, and if they
were "Whitey's guys", why wasn't he arrested along with
them? These were the questions being asked by Whitey's

apologists, and they seemed to be valid, as Bulger continued to ply his trade on the streets of South Boston for four more years. When the truth was finally made known in the years after 1995, the year Bulger went on the run, and the enormity of his crimes couldn't be ignored nor defended, I asked myself why I had so passionately justified Whitey's reputation and why its preservation had become so personal. Although we were friendly, we weren't friends, and his social skills were far from charismatic. I was not one to be star-struck nor did I want to hang around him; in fact, I avoided him as much as possible. I know there are people who admire or even envy the outlaw, the guy who won't conform, makes his own rules, and thumbs his nose at authority. But I'm not one of those; in fact, I find a structured environment much more inviting. Why then did I compulsively defend him?

I made Whitey's reputation personal because it was personal on a couple of levels. I desperately wanted him to be as I perceived him; as a person who cared for the neighborhood and for those who inhabited it. As a guy who looked out for the weak and the elderly, and who was able to get things done by circumventing the bureaucracy and cutting through the red tape that frustrates and so often defeats the people who live in the neighborhoods. He was from my generation and espoused the same code that I lived by and believed in with all my heart; a code that emphasized loyalty, friendship, taking care of your own, and keeping your mouth shut. I had long since lost my naiveté and had become very cynical of people and their motives. I needed Whitey to be what he professed to be; I needed these principles to mean something. If he was the man the media described, I abided by a set of values that were so false as to be mythic and were just hollow words used by those few in power for their own ends. Secondly,

I prided myself in discerning what made people tick, and if Bulger proved to be an informer and a drug dealer, then I was fooled completely. Maybe I so badly wanted him to be genuine, I fooled myself.

Sometimes he just wanted to talk. There were a handful of times when Whitey would show up by himself at closing time and begin a conversation—to be more precise, a monologue. A conversation with him was an exercise in listening. I recall the night he gave me a tutorial on methods of corruption. If the target was someone who wasn't susceptible to intimidation for whatever reason, maybe he was a prominent individual or one who had too many friends in high places, Bulger would come at him in one of a couple of ways. He might create a problem for him and then solve it. For instance, if this person was in law enforcement working a drug case, Whitey would inform him there was a hit out on him and mention the name of a guy who had a reputation as a psycho as the one who was after him. He'd then tell the target that he didn't think it was right because he knew he was a fair guy with a young family, and he was trying to get them to call off the whole thing by calling in some favors the drug guys owed him. Whitey would tell him it was going to be tough but he would do his best. A week or two later, he would tell the guy that, although it wasn't easy, he was able to get the hit called off. Once the quarry accepted Whitey's help and even if nothing in return was asked for immediately, he now owed Whitey a favor. It was like money in the bank.

A second method was to open up a line of communication with the person, which was, usually, welcomed by the target because they naively believed they could elicit information from Whitey. In the process of their conversations, he would discover what the person liked to do recreationally. If the guy was a runner, he would purchase him a pair of running shoes, or if he liked fine dining, he might buy him a nice bottle of wine. If he accepted the gift, next time Whitey would up the ante and, as he told me, "then I owned him." I thought, at the time, these stories to be apocryphal and most likely based on a number of similar but separate events, but I trust the machinations—methods Machiavelli might have envied—were applied by Whitey in exactly the ways he described.

On one particular night, I was struck by his mood. Whitey's demeanor was usually calm and unemotional or angry and demonstrative, but on this night he seemed deeply disturbed. He didn't speak for the longest time, so I went about my business of reconciling the daily receipts and making out a bank deposit slip so I could drop the money into the night depository on the way home. Normally if he came in at closing, I would be in for a long night, but he didn't show any interest in having a conversation, so I assumed we would be leaving shortly. I asked him how he was doing and he answered, "I'm thinking of retiring." I suppressed a smile because the word "retire" associated with Bulger always reminded me of when he turned sixty-five and applied for and began to collect Social Security and how ironic it was that the federal government was laundering money for him by giving him a legitimate source of income. He went on to say it was time to enjoy himself and that he was going to sail around the world and that he had been researching boats and had even been to inspect a few in person. Nothing came of this, but I often wonder if Whitey was reacting to information he received pertaining to the grand jury that eventually indicted him or that John Connolly had to retire from the F.B.I. leaving Whitey on his own. This occurred in 1993 or 1994, about a year or a year and a half before he went on the run. He may have known the clock was counting down.

On another occasion, I was looking forward to going home when Whitey rapped to be let in. I let him in and relocked the door. I had shut off the lights before he entered, so we stood in the dark at the double doors facing out onto Old Colony Avenue, neither of us speaking. It was a severely frigid winter's night, and as the headlights from an occasional passing car reflected eerily off the snow banks along the deserted avenue, they cast a surreal light into the store which quickly faded, leaving us once again in darkness.

Whitey broke the silence bringing up the name of Paulie McGonagle. Paulie was a few years older than me, but we grew up on the same corner and had shared quite a few experiences. We were in numerous barroom brawls and gang fights together, most of which he instigated. We competed with and against each other in sports, and together we drank many beers on many occasions. In fact, I celebrated with him on the day he was found not guilty on a charge of armed robbery with shots fired. Paulie and I had a history; he even tried to kill me one night.

Paulie was a Mullen and one of the survivors of a shooting war versus the Killeen crew with whom Whitey Bulger was allied. When Killeen was killed, a truce was called and the Mullens joined forces with Bulger and took over the rackets in South Boston. Given the personalities involved and that there were lots of chiefs and very few Indians, it didn't seem to be an arrangement that could be sustained. It wasn't—during the next few years, a number of Mullens went missing or turned up dead. Bulger was left standing.

On this particular night, Paulie had been dead for a number of years, although in legal terms he was listed as missing because they hadn't found a body. Whitey soon cleared up any doubts I may have had concerning Paulie's mortality. He began by saying Paulie had a big mouth and was always stirring up trouble, which I took to mean he was bad-mouthing Whitey. If you talked about Bulger, the odds were he'd hear about it, and he always retaliated. He then told me "Paulie had to go." These words immediately put me on the defensive because I didn't understand why he would tell me this. My only reasoning was he knew I was once a Mullen and had been friends with Paulie, and he was testing my reaction to detect if I might pose any danger to him, or telling me about Paulie's death was a warning to keep my mouth shut. Whatever his reason, I forced myself to look him in the eyes and struggled to not give away any sign of disapproval as he continued his story. It didn't hurt that we were virtually standing in the dark.

Whitey said they told Paulie they had some of the best counterfeit bills they had ever seen, and they wanted him to take a look at them. (Paulie had been passing counterfeit money for years.) Throughout the telling, Whitey used the pronoun "they", but never mentioned any names. Kevin Weeks states in his book *Brutal* that Tom King was the other half of "they." They pulled up to the curb, Paulie climbed onto the backseat and they drove somewhere and parked. He was handed a briefcase, which he opened, expecting to see stacks of counterfeit bills; instead he saw nothing but an empty briefcase. For that split second before they opened fire, he must have known what was about to come down. They must have gone through his pockets since Whitey told me Paulie had been looking forward to a good weekend because he had a plastic baggie full of uppers with him. I don't know why Paulie was killed, but if I had to guess, I would think it had something to do with Donnie McGonagle. Donnie was Paulie's brother, and Whitey shot him to death, mistaking him for Paulie, and even though I don't think Paulie was capable of shooting anyone, Bulger had to perceive him as a potential threat. Paulie's mouth would have given him an excuse. Whitey usually tied up loose ends.

I am haunted still by the vision of Paulie peering into that empty briefcase and the feelings of dread and fear and helplessness that must have flooded his mind in that moment just before they ended his life. There are times when I read about a particular murder Bulger committed and wonder how one human being can perform such an act and carry it out, not in the heat of passion, but in cold blood and devoid of any emotion. How can one sit at a kitchen table or in a car or on a living room sofa and painstakingly plan the taking of a human life? I find myself ranking the murders in terms of their brutality, if that's even possible. I think of the two girls garroted to death and then grieve for John McIntyre, who asked to be shot so to put an end to his agony, and see Paulie's empty briefcase, but as disturbing as these particular images are to me, there are countless others who are haunted by their own images of their loved ones', friends,' and relatives' last moments occasioned by one man's megalomania, unrestrained power, and lack of conscience.

The impact of the Whitey Bulger phenomenon will be long lasting and far reaching. It will prove to be more than a footnote in the folklore of South Boston or to be trivialized into tall tales swapped in the neighborhood bars by old-timers bragging of how well they knew him or about the night they told him off or the beating they witnessed him administer to Joe Blow or how he had always liked and respected them. There will be college courses offered on the impact of Bulger's ability to corrupt the

F.B.I. and law students will complete their doctorate on the case and its many facets. I am curious to know the individuals Bulger informed on, because I find it fascinating how much information has been reported flowing to and not from Whitey or Stevie Flemmi. We'll have to wait awhile before that becomes public knowledge if at all.

It seems to me the effect on the legal system will be huge as the guidelines dealing with informants will be or already have been narrowed and will be fastidiously adhered to, causing a drop off in useful intelligence. Defense attorneys will play the corruption card more often to a jury who is more likely to agree. Judges are becoming more cynical and beginning to scrutinize testimony and evidence from law enforcement, prosecutors, and even the evidence labs very closely. We live in a society that distrusts the government, a country where one-third of its population believes the United States government was either involved in 9/11 or was aware it was about to occur and where fifty-seven percent of its citizens are positive that J.F.K. was the victim of a conspiracy that included our intelligence organizations and higher-ups in our own government. This is the real tragedy of the Bulger/ Flemmi/ Connolly/ F.B.I. fiasco; it reinforces the conspiracy theorists' cynicism and it plants doubts in the minds of the people who trust and believe in the basic goodness of the system even if individuals occasionally prostitute it. Hitler's reputation will be rehabilitated before the F.B.I. will regain a modicum of the respect squandered by a handful of ambitious, selfish individuals.

Maybe this sordid chapter in our legal system is the very corrective action needed to rebalance the scales of justice, but for good or ill, the system will be changed forever.

CHAPTER 9

THE WORST OF TIMES

*T*he event I had anticipated finally occurred in the late summer of 1991 when I was subpoenaed to testify before a grand jury convened to investigate Whitey Bulger. I had evidence that the government was paying me more attention by the strange clicks on my telephone and an envelope I found in my post office box one afternoon. It was addressed to the REGIONAL CHIEF POSTAL INSPECTOR-NORTHEAST REGION, Newark, New Jersey. Inside was a second envelope marked as RESTRICTED INFORMATION that contained a form entitled RESTRICTED INFORMATION CON-CERNING MAIL MATTER, and on this form was a list of the mail I had received a day or two before. I don't know if the post office simply put the envelope in my box by mistake or a friend of mine who worked in that partic-ular branch put it there as a warning. But either way I received it, and it offered certain proof the government was monitoring my mail.

As further evidence, after closing the store one night, I was drinking in Triple O's when the security alarm com-pany called to say the silent alarm had gone off in the package store. I drove to the store, entered, looked around, and having found nothing out of the ordinary, I reset the alarm and returned to the bar. After about ten minutes the alarm company called again, and I drove back to the store and searched it again without any result. This sequence of events was repeated two or three more times before the telephone calls ceased. My thoughts were a mouse or a rat had set off the motion detector and caused the alarm to activate. I erased the incident from mind until two or three days later when I noticed a cardboard carton placed on the top shelf of our liquor display blocking a security camera we had installed. This particular camera was placed so as to record the activity at the cash register. Since this camera had been installed, we had caught two employees stealing cash, so I immediately reached up and removed the carton. When I came to work the next afternoon, I noticed the carton was once again placed on the shelf, blocking the camera. The incident with the security alarms of a few nights earlier came to mind, and I put the two events together. The alarm was set off by law enforcement tapping into our security camera, and someone had warned us of the situation which explained the carton blocking the camera.

Due to these occurrences and a general sense of uneasiness, the issuance of my subpoena came as no surprise. My lawyer, Danny Rull, whom I still consider a friend and whose character belies the popularly accepted view of the legal profession, negotiated with the government to grant me some form of immunity. My understanding was I couldn't be charged with any crime except perjury, and I may be charged with contempt of court if I refused to answer any question. The subpoena summoned not only my appearance but all the financial records of the liquor store.

On the morning of my scheduled appearance, Danny arrived at my apartment with a van, and we made two or three trips up and down the elevator, loading carton after carton of ledgers, cancelled checks, check registers, and I don't know what else into the van. When we arrived at the federal court house, we were met by a federal marshal who made a point of calling me Bo, my nickname, instead of my given name, Gordon. I took this as another example of the scare tactics used by some law enforcement officers who consider themselves more intelligent than most. I assume he was attempting to deliver the message that he knew all about me. I am not denying I was nervous because I was—very nervous. However, if there is one thing that gets my competitive juices flowing, it's when someone attempts to outthink me, and this marshal did me a big favor by calling me Bo. I entered the grand jury room very relaxed and ready for anything. The questioning went well, and except for a couple of contentious moments, the Assistant United States Attorney who questioned me was respectful and a gentleman. My sense, however, was this line of questioning was meant to lay the groundwork for a second appearance, which would take place after they had reviewed the volumes of records we had released into their custody that morning. There would be more to come.

Beginning in late 1992, the volume of the store's sales began a steady downward trend that required a periodic influx of cash. Kevin O'Neil and I were both reinvesting as the need arose. The factors that contributed to the decrease in sales were, as I saw them, the reduction of cocaine sales and the ethnic change in the neighborhood. A great majority of our sales depended on the two housing projects that bordered the store, and anything that impacted them financially greatly affected our sales.

Beginning with the mass drug bust in August of 1990, cocaine sales all but dried up. This had a two-fold impact; first the money the sellers were making was no longer available, and secondly the neighborhood wasn't using as much cocaine, so they didn't consume as much alcohol. I don't intend to paint the whole neighborhood with the same brush. The cocaine users tended to be the younger generation and were certainly the minority. The other and most important, change was a difference in the drinking habits of the new inhabitants of the housing projects and therefore a huge impact on our bottom line. Our average customer, before the integration of the housing projects, purchased a six-pack of beer per day Monday through Thursday and an eighteen-pack (a "suitcase") on Friday and/or Saturday nights. These sales translated into $5.50 times four or $22.00 from Monday through Thursday and an additional $18.50 per suitcase on the weekend. The alcohol of choice of our newer customers was forty-ounce bottles of fortified beer (beer with added alcohol content) that sold for $1.50 per bottle. So just do the math and you can see the direction our sales were going.

Except for the continuing erosion of our business and the obvious escalating activity of law enforcement in the area, the next couple of years were utopian in retrospect. It seemed that even the news media had their fill of Whitey's adventures. After all, how many stories could be squeezed out of the relationship of the Bulger brothers, the cocaine crackdown, or the lottery windfall? I still held on to the dream of selling the business/building and moving on, contrary to my every instinct that told me to face reality. Things had gone too far, bridges had been burned, and money and mistakes had to be repaid. I think I knew this was the one act in my life when I couldn't just exit stage right as I had on so many other occasions. There would be consequences.

This period did host another and much more contentious grand jury appearance in November 1995. As I had deduced, my first subpoena was to gather the financial records of the liquor store and the purchase of the business and the building, and now the government had had the time to study the sequence of events and the numbers and to devise a game plan. The questioning was tough and the AUSA wasn't playing the "good cop" role. He came after me pretty good. Once again, I had immunity from self-incrimination but not from perjury, but this time around, I had another danger to factor into the equation.

By now, I was pretty sure Whitey and John Connolly were more than just acquaintances, and if my instinct for survival served me as it had in the past, there was an excellent chance Whitey would be aware of my testimony within a matter of days. Now, if I was asked the right or, according to which side you were on, the wrong question under oath, I had a real dilemma. Do I lie and face five years in prison or tell the truth and take a bullet in the head? I had decided to save the boys the price of a bullet and take my chances with prison. But if the truth be known, I would have opted for perjuring myself regardless of the potential danger because I had an aversion to informing. Joan and I had this conversation a few days before my scheduled grand jury appearance when I told her of my decision to risk prison time rather than inform. I joked with her that I could use the vacation.

My choice not to inform is in no way a condemnation of anyone who goes another route. Every situation and its circumstances are unique, and I try very hard not to judge the actions of others. I have enough trouble living by my own conscience without trying to foster my values on anyone else. And by the grace of God, although I skirted a number of questions, I never perjured myself. The next day, however, I received a call from my lawyer telling me the AUSA had accused me of perjury and I would be subpoenaed again. I think this was a scare tactic because I was "invited" to a third and fourth grand jury but I was never indicted.

Maybe two or three times in one's life a pivotal event occurs, a turning point that changes everything, perhaps for good, perhaps for ill. January 5, 1995 was one of those days. It was like any other day, until I met Kevin Weeks outside of the Rotary Variety store at about 10:30 that night, when he told me that indictments had come down and Stevie Flemmi had been arrested and Whitey was on the run. My first reaction was "here we go again." The media attention, increased law enforcement presence, more grand juries, the questions from friends and relatives would multiply exponentially and with them the ultimate side effects of the glare of unwanted publicity and the embarrassment the families would have to endure. Little did I imagine the far-reaching effects Whitey's disappearance and Stevie's arrest would have on not only me but on so many others. The great and terrible Oz had fled to Kansas or to other regions unknown, leaving dozens of believers stranded in the Emerald city to face the consequences.

If the last couple of years were a relative calm before the storm, ominous clouds were forming on the horizon and heading my way. If anything, my alcohol consumption was increasing. I drank every night after work and then spent all day Sunday in bed with a gigantic hangover. Our business was declining steadily, and it was becoming more and more difficult to pay the money owed each week. I had long since lost control of my anger, and it exploded at the most unexpected times, completely taking me by surprise. My mood alternated between acute anxiety and deep depression, and there were many days when I had to literally grasp my ankles with my hands and place them on the floor in order to force myself to get out of bed. I began to retreat into the only place I felt safe—deep within myself—putting a great strain on my relationship with Joan.

It seemed there was a new crisis every day, a new hole in the dam that needed plugging, and I was running out of fingers. The liquor sales were steadily declining. and two or three times a week, I had to deposit my personal money in order to pay the bills. Never one to plan for the future, personal money was in fact borrowed money. I began with credit cards until they reached their limits, when, of course, the credit card companies would increase my credit limit, and competing companies would issue me new cards with a $10,000 limit. As the business worsened and the years went by, I owed well over $150,000 at 25% interest. Yet I still held to my unrealistic, illogical dream of weathering the storm and to sell the business/building, providing me with a new start. As the credit card money reached its limits, I began to borrow from friends and relatives.

My day began with a phone call to an automated service the bank provided which would give me the balance in the store's checking account; this was before all banking business was available on the Internet. The data was usually accessible around 6 a.m., giving me all of an hour and a half of sleep because I would have drank until about 4:30 a.m. As I dialed the telephone, the anxiety would begin in the pit of my stomach, and the adrenaline would course through my body with such intensity my hands would shake so violently I had to grasp the phone with both hands. On those rare days the checking account revealed a positive balance, I felt a sense of relief comparable to being told the tumor was a cyst after all. Conversely, when the account was overdrawn, I hung up the phone and began to run down a mental checklist of possible sources of money that would allow me to survive for one more day, at least until tomorrow. It was out of the question for the store to be put on the "list" for non-payment of liquor bills because we would have to pay cash for any further deliveries, which was, in effect, a death notice for the business and for any hope I may have of a future.

By this time I had lost my pride and was borrowing from anyone and everyone. In retrospect, I was running my own pyramid scheme, although it wasn't planned and I really intended to repay every debt. Joan closed out her retirement account, my ex-wife Peggy remortgaged her house, and I used the proceeds to pay off most of my debts, but within a few months I had used the paid-off credit cards to keep the store alive by running up my cards to over $150,000 again. To my eternal shame, I still owe my son $9,000 and three friends over $35,000. I even ran up my partner's line of credit to $30,000. Needless to say, there have been many sleepless nights spent trying to come up with a plan to repay these people who were once my friends. By the way, it is important to note not a penny of this money did I use for personal expenses. It was all invested in the business and/or used for legal representation.

The other shoe dropped in late 1999, when Kevin Weeks and my partner Kevin O'Neil were arrested and charged with racketeering after being indicted by a federal grand jury. The month before our last chance to come out of this situation whole died when a federal judge blocked the sale of the building and business that I had negotiated with a lady who owned a Laundromat next to our property. The agreed-upon price was $850,000, which would have satisfied our debts and restored my peace of mind. I felt bad for the lady, who I think was Vietnamese, because the government subpoenaed her to a grand jury and really frightened her. She was questioned on whether we had forced her into the purchase and/or was acting as a "straw." A straw being defined as someone who owns something in name only, fronting for the actual owners. To her credit, she stuck to the truth and didn't agree to their accusations out of fear or intimidation. This was the first inkling I had that the government had a keen interest in the property, and this action by the federal courts certainly didn't bode well for my financial future.

The emotional and financial pressure from so many sources was beginning to overwhelm me. My personal finances were in a mess. I was trying to support Peggy and to pull my weight with Joan's and my living expenses, which was becoming more difficult because of the number of weeks I was unable to draw a salary from the store due to decreasing sales. I was living off credit cards. The liquor sales continued to decrease, and now there was the additional responsibility of providing my partner's family with a week's pay while he was incarcerated.

Every morning posed the potential of not meeting the store's expenses, and the anticipation of what challenge the next day may bring made for some sleepless nights even with the amount of alcohol I consumed. Any day could deliver another subpoena to another grand jury or even an arrest. I thought my telephone was tapped, and I knew my mail was being monitored, not to mention watching for trailing automobiles. Shortly before Kevin Weeks was arrested, he and I were standing outside of the liquor store when he noticed an airplane circling our block. I am terrible at estimating distances, but the plane seemed only a speck. It circled for a half hour and only flew off when Kevin drove away. I can only assume it had some parabolic listening device and was attempting to eavesdrop on Kevin's conversations. This was serious stuff law enforcement was throwing at these guys.

As I have previously stated, I was filled with anxiety and/or depression, and my anger was uncontrollable and would explode for no apparent reason, taking even me by surprise. My coping mechanism, besides alcohol, was to withdraw from those around me and from life in general. This sort of behavior doesn't exactly endear one to others relationally, and I was pushing Joan to the limit of her patience and endurance. We've all heard of living one day at a time; well, my compartmentalization was in half-hour increments. If I could get my mind off my troubles for a half hour, I obtained enough relief to face the next catastrophe.

Things were bad and becoming worse. Although I didn't have a specific plan for suicide, I knew it was the ultimate solution if that light at the end of the tunnel that I was constantly searching for proved to be just another train. Strangely, knowing death would put an end to my problems somehow gave me some hope and a semblance of peace.

The hoped-for light was, in fact, a speeding locomotive in the form of a civil suit that, at long last, shattered any dream that I may have had for some kind of "happy" ending to this nightmare.

Sometime in late 1983, Whitey and Kevin Weeks purchased a liquor store from a local guy and his wife. Kevin's version of the story—and one that I choose to believe because he was under great pressure from the government to tell the truth or forfeit a clemency deal and serve a possible life sentence—was that the guy had approached them and asked if they were interested in purchasing the store. They agreed on a price and took over the store. The seller's version was that Whitey, Kevin, and Stevie Flemmi had extorted the store from them at gunpoint with their two young daughters present.[8]

Seventeen years later, Julie Dammers, the now divorced wife of the former owner, was suing to regain the liquor store and obtain the building which they never owned. With Whitey on the run and Kevin Weeks in prison and the fear of retaliation virtually nonexistent, it seemed someone was suing someone on a daily basis. The first I had heard of the alleged extortion was in a newspaper article, and my initial reaction to the suit was I hadn't any knowledge of or participation in the purchase, and secondly the six-year statute of limitations had certainly run its course. Guess again. The judge ruled against us because Dammers and her ex-husband had remained under duress long after the passage of the statute of limitations.

The judge's ruling was a devastating body blow. I was barely keeping current with my attorney, John Bonistalli's, billing and with the additional hours that would be required with the current suit, I was ready to settle the case quickly. I simply didn't have the resources to fight very long. But the decision to settle was made impossible by Julie Dammers' attorney. Enter Attorney Paul Gannon. He made it very clear from the outset that he expected to win the case and consequently the liquor store and building without any compensation to my creditors or me. He left me no choice but to fight to the bitter end, for if I settled on his terms, I would spend less on attorney's

[8] Reference *Brutal* by Kevin Weeks and Phyllis Karas, Chapter 10

fees but would owe about $250,000 for liquor bills and taxes.

Attorney Gannon is a unique individual, and I could never decide whether he was incompetent or simply mean spirited. He seemed to glory in alienating people. He and his client were in a perfect place. They only had to wait out the criminal procedures and the government would have seized my property, and with some negotiation they would have been awarded the business/building with little or no work. One day I was in discussion with a federal official and mentioned attorney Gannon believed he would gain the property with little or no compensation. The official told me that if we lost in court or I settled without compensation, the government would put a lien on the property and force Gannon to continue the suit with them.

As I had stated, I was giving Kevin O'Neil's family his paycheck while he was incarcerated. I volunteered the fact that I was paying Kevin during one of the many depositions attorney Gannon demanded. He immediately went to the newspapers with the story and began contempt of court proceedings against Kevin O'Neil and me.

I'd like to quote some portions of AUSA Richard L. Hoffman's filing to the United States District Court in regards to attorney Gannon's contempt proceedings: AUSA Hoffman wrote, *"Stripped of their hyperbole and taken in light of McIntyre's sworn and documented response, Movants' allegations simply cannot establish clearly and convincingly that the challenged expenditures by McIntyre were so extraordinary and so different from the payments and payment practices followed by the business before the entry of the Supplemental Restraining Order, that a reasonable person in McIntyre's position, in charge of the Business's day-to-day operations, clearly would have known that his actions violated the Supplemental Restraining Order."*

If I may ask the reader's indulgence and quote one additional paragraph, actually a footnote, from AUSA Hoffman: *Notably, one major expense confronting McIntyre and the business since the issuance of the restraining order, has been the cost of defending Movants' civil lawsuit. Movants could have waited, and now should wait, to press their claims to the business in the ancillary forfeiture proceedings in this case, or in the Weeks criminal cases whichever first occur. If Movants had awaited the proper time to assert their claim to the Business in the proper federal forum, that would have avoided the significant and apparently unwarranted and unjustified dissipation of their own and the Business's assets occasioned by their lawsuit.* The motion for Commencement of Contempt Proceeding was dismissed. Neither the court's finding nor the advice of AUSA Hoffman contained in his filing on this matter deterred attorney Gannon, and with full speed ahead, he cost me and his client a great deal of money. I don't profess to know much about the law and its nuances, but I do know if a little common sense and communication were applied, both sides of this suit could have avoided a needless waste of time and money.

I was at the end of my financial tether. I had to make one of the toughest decisions of my life, a decision that stripped me of the little pride I had left. After agonizing over my calculations, I hadn't any choice but bankruptcy. For about a week, I thought a lot about suicide, and only the realization of leaving my family and Joan with the mess I had made nullified that course of action. Ironically it was attorney Gannon's stridency and combativeness that restored and reinvigorated my resolve to see this entire sordid affair to its ultimate conclusion whatever the outcome.

I filed for bankruptcy under Chapter 13 in the effort to salvage what little self-esteem I had left. Chapter 13 allows a plan to repay some percentage of your outstanding debts; I think it's about 25%. Of course, attorney Gannon hired a bankruptcy attorney to be at my hearing with the judge to accuse me of filing a fraudulent claim so as to hinder Ms. Dammers' civil suit. The judge disagreed and granted me Chapter 13 protection. Eventually, as my financial situation worsened over the next three years, I filed for and was granted full bankruptcy protection under Chapter 7.

I was flat broke and could no longer pay the mortgage on my wife's home, forcing Peggy to sell. The sale of the house netted about $57,800, of which, my half went to my creditors under Chapter 13 less some $9,000 that I gave to Peggy. Joan was supporting me, except for the few checks I could get from the liquor store. The store was not supporting itself and I had nothing left to keep it going, so I finally gave up the ghost and shut it down in May of 2001.

At the risk of boring the reader with the legal machinations that followed, I think it important to note that the closing of the store began a countdown because the store's liquor license would be revoked within a certain time period. After the licensing board granted a couple of extensions, they set a final date for December 15, 2001 for an agreement to be reached. This deadline may have been the impetus for an agreement and this tortured procedure to finally end. Ms. Dammers consented to pay any outstanding corporate and real estate taxes, to negotiate the payment of the liquor bills with the various distributors, to pay any utilities in arrears, and to settle the remainder of my attorney's fees. The total was somewhere between $200,000 and $250,000. I would have settled for the same deal a year and a half earlier.

The final irony occurred at a hearing at the City of Boston Licensing Board that was held to transfer the liquor license to Ms. Dammers. One of the ex-politicians who sat on the licensing board highly praised attorney Gannon for the great job he did in restoring the business to Ms. Dammers. The chairman then officially transferred the liquor license from my corporation to Ms. Dammers, Paul Gannon, and a third person who, I believe, worked in attorney Gannon's law office. I don't know what their agreement was, but it seems to me Ms. Dammers had acquired a couple of partners somewhere in the process.

After sixteen years of extraordinarily hard work, emotional turmoil, physical danger, legal difficulties, and financial disaster, it was finished. I began to breathe again.

CHAPTER 10

ARE WE HOME YET?

*M*onths after closing the store, I found myself still waiting for my inner turmoil to subside, and to find some semblance of peace. I was as withdrawn as ever, and my alcohol consumption hadn't lessened. It seemed most of the people I knew were in similar situations. They were struggling financially to keep their heads above water; trying to keep their kids on the right path; expending most of their time and energy on just making a living, just getting by, just surviving for one more day; and, like me, fleeing on the escape route of self-medication. For the first time in many, many years, I had time to reflect on my life and its meaning. My first thoughts were—Is this all there is? Is this all we can expect out of this thing we call life? I wanted more.

Joan felt the same. Our differences were that while I thought about it, she acted on it. While my idea of peace was being alone, Joan wanted to engage. She was concerned about her (our) drinking and began to attend AA. At about the same time, she began to shop around for a church where she could feel comfortable. I'm not sure where her desire to attend church came from, because since I'd known her, she professed to not believe there was a God. Maybe it was AA espousing a higher power, but I choose to believe it was a whispering from God.

She visited most, if not all, the churches in the area. I halfheartedly accompanied her two or three times, but I didn't think the answer to my questions would come by attending a church. After all, didn't church consist of people, and I saw people as the source of, not the solution to, my problems.

A girl who attended AA with Joan recommended a church that met in the local high school, and when Joan's friend mentioned she could wear jeans and that it had great music, she was sold. My curiosity was piqued after hearing Joan's glowing reports of the pastor's sermons, the worship music, and the overall experience of the service. Joan only had good things to say about most things, but there was something about her reaction to this church that was different. There was a certain excitement about her as she related the pastor's latest message and how it seemed to be aimed specifically at her. She brought home audio tapes of the sermon for me to hear, and not wanting to sound interested, I'd tell her I would try to get to them if I had time. Whenever I was alone at home or in my car, I would play them, and I discovered that Joan was mistaken. The sermons were directed at me, not at her. I was, however, very wary about becoming involved in this church thing on many levels, not the least of which was my reluctance to be a member of any group, especially a Christian group, where I would have to react with people without the uninhibiting effect of alcohol.

It soon became very clear that Joan was close to being totally committed to the church and was seriously seeking God. I, on the other hand, was becoming jealous. If Joan went all in and I didn't join her, I knew one of two things would happen. Either I would do my best to poison her attitude toward the church, or we would grow apart and I would eventually lose her entirely. South Shore Community Church was a small group-based church, and Joan had joined a group two or three months after joining the church. My competition had now doubled, as had my concern for our relationship. I knew I had to get involved or be left behind, and so, after playing "hard to get," I granted Joan a "favor" and, for all the wrong reasons, agreed to accompany her to church one eventful Sunday morning. I wish I could say the rest was history, but nothing in which I was involved came easy in those days.

It was the best of days and the worst of days. My anxiety level was so high, my hands were shaking, and when I became anxious I hated the world and everyone in it. I'm sure I made a great impression on Joan's friends as she introduced me to what seemed to me to be a hundred people. Even today I'm uncomfortable with small talk and will only speak when I have something to say. Well, factor in my being somewhere I didn't want to be, with people whom I didn't want to be with, and my uneasiness quotient increased tenfold, which must have been quite evident to anyone whom I met. The church was meeting in the old Bridgewater-Raynham High School at the time, and I couldn't wait to get to my seat, which represented some modicum of isolation, a small island of required silence and a large sense of relief.

The worship music was contemporary Christian and since I hadn't yet learned to appreciate its emotional power, I simply tolerated it and silently questioned why I had allowed myself to be in such an uncomfortable situation. Why hadn't I just stayed home? The ensuing thirty or so minutes answered my question. The pastor, Rob Reimer, delivered a sermon that devastated me with its simple truth and powerful conviction. Its theme was forgiveness and I thought, "Here it comes"—more Christian rules that are impossible to follow and only serve to condemn and cause the listener to feel guilty because he can't live up to an impossible standard. If he said anything about "turning thy other cheek," I think I would have walked out and never looked back. Where I came from the only cheek turned was the one you hit with a right-hand punch. Much to my surprise and bewilderment, Pastor Rob was advocating forgiveness for the benefit of the injured party, not for the offender. He described how you may be in turmoil, rehearsing what you were going to say to someone who had sinned against you, while he was at peace, unaware of your agitation. The pastor's talk forced me to question a value that I held as unimpeachable. My peers insisted you must never let anyone get away with showing you any disrespect, and I spent a great deal of my life filled with anger and bitterness caused by any real or imagined insult. I could hardly wait to get home so that I could research the scriptural passages Pastor Rob had quoted during his talk. This one sermon had awakened distant memories of a long- forgotten God and the stirring of a longing for His truth and knowledge. A seed had been planted, and it slowly began to sprout, slowly at first, but growing nevertheless.

Week after week Rob's sermons assailed the values that I had lived by, and the very logic of his teachings forced me to rethink my definition of right and wrong. His words conflicted with everything I held as virtuous. I sorely wanted to deny them and label them as just so much rhetoric. I mean he was telling me that pride was a sin, not something to strive for and to cherish. What? Wasn't sin simply the Ten Commandments? When did audacity, ambition, or affluence get on the list? Aren't they human traits much to be desired? After the Sunday sermon my head would be spinning, and I would hurry home to my Bible, hoping to disprove what I had just heard. Invariably the pastor's words accurately cited scripture, and once again I would be overwhelmed by the truth and the logic of the sermon. More often my thoughts would take me back to the time before I decided to choose the world instead of God. If only I had a Pastor Rob to guide and teach me God's truth, how different my life may have been.

I began to attend church regularly, and after avoiding it as long as I could, I joined the small group in which Joan was a member. In the beginning I was my uncommunicative, withdrawn self. But soon my longing to have more of God compelled me to shed my shell, and thereafter I gave the impression that I was being argumentative and combative. John and Maggie Littlefield led our group, and after observing my attitude at our weekly meetings, I would have given anything to listen in as they discussed their newest member in the privacy of their own home.

I was thirsting to know more of God, to understand His ways, to learn everything He wanted me to learn, and I wanted our small-group meetings to be dedicated to teaching me. Unfortunately the anxiety I experienced in any social setting was elevated by the hunger that was compelling me to know more of God. Most members of our small group interpreted my passion as anger, and I became increasingly more aware that I was making the others uncomfortable. Once again I proved to be awkward and ill at ease in a group surrounding, but for a different and complete opposite reason. Instead of too little, this time I said too much. I soon resigned from the small group.

Now the Sunday sermon and scripture were my only contacts with God (I was struggling with prayer), and although I was still attending church, I didn't have any meaningful relationship with the congregation nor did I desire any. Whenever I was around the "church people," a title I bestowed on the church community, my antenna was up. Joan and I were not yet married, and I was just waiting for an excuse to leave the church. If I heard so much as a whisper of criticism, I would have exited without looking back. But much to my disbelief, we were never judged. That is not to say we weren't taught God's plan for a man and a woman. For instance, one night during our small-group meeting, John Littlefield took me aside and suggested Joan and I abstain from sex until we were married. It took a great deal of courage for John to confront me, and I will always admire him for it.

It seemed every sermon that Rob Reimer preached changed me or at least redirected my thinking from worldly thoughts to God's truths. I couldn't get enough of his teaching and the Word. Joan and I came to Christ and were eventually married in the church, and it has become a most important part of our lives.

I couldn't get enough. I virtually devoured the Bible and listened to Rob's sermons again and again, but I soon realized I needed community to gain new insight and to have a group to discuss the Word and listen to their witness and Godly experiences. I rejoined our small group with my tail tucked between my legs. Some members of the small group, who are now dear friends, were not particularly overjoyed with my return.

I'm afraid I continued to intimidate others because my passion was mistaken for anger and because of my grave, humorless, stern demeanor. Janet Hale, now a dear friend, would ask others why someone as sweet as Joan was involved with someone as angry as me, and if the truth be known, I wondered the same. As deep as my faith and conviction in Christ was, I still possessed a heart that I, above all, protected from emotional hurt. I was overly sensitive to criticism and would push back whenever I heard or imagined I heard any negative words, further reinforcing an image of me as angry and argumentative. As much as I wanted to change and to be more like Christ, it was so difficult to shed my old self after sixty years of carefully crafting a persona whose main objective was to keep everyone at a safe distance. To the casual observer I hadn't changed, but inside, where I had hidden for much of my life, there was a metamorphosis taking place. It was both scary and exciting. On one hand I was afraid to let go of my old self, and on the other I knew Christ offered my only chance for real freedom. The world tenders its hopes and dreams as a carrot on a stick dangling just out of our reach, and only when we discern the futility of chasing after its earthly treasures can we begin to accept the Gospel and the incredible impact it can have on our lives.

The first year of my walk with Christ was exhilarating. It seemed each time I read scripture, a new truth was revealed to me. My awe for Jesus was overwhelming, and I immersed myself in His Word and Christian literature to better know Him. I began to write Christian poetry, Christian-based essays, and I even wrote a play depicting my take on Judas Iscariot.

In the first few months of my rebirth came the fire of commitment. I was convicted to aid someone, evangelize, volunteer in a food kitchen, tithe, or spend time with the elderly, the teens, or the children. I felt the need to honor Christ by doing something, anything. This proved to be less than fulfilling as I volunteered for various ministries that fit neither my skills nor my personality and for which God certainly didn't call me.

It was during this time that I learned a lesson, and the lesson was to wait. I'm now comfortable with the voice of the Holy Spirit, and although I'm not qualified to proclaim my experience as a universal truth, I do know how God has used me. Just when the fervor of rebirth was at its hottest and I was driven to do something for others and for God, the Holy Spirit was prompting me to wait. This was a time I needed to concentrate on me, to invest myself in scripture and to recognize the promptings of the Spirit. I was not yet weaned from milk nor was I ready for solid foods. God has never used me when I took on kingdom tasks of my own volition, only when in obedience to a Holy Spirit prompting.

I wanted more. I began to chase Christ's promises, and my prayer life was concentrated on them. Since I knew Christ always keeps His promises, I went after them with all my being. The Holy Spirit kept leading me to Matthew 7:7,8 and Luke 11:9,10— "Ask and it will be given to you; seek and you will find; knock and the door will be opened to you. For EVERYONE who asks receives; He who seeks finds; and to HIM who knocks, the door will be opened." I found these verses fascinating. I wanted a personal relationship with God; an occasional pat on the back or even a scolding. I was seeking any contact that would reassure me that God had an interest in my life and a place for me in His Kingdom. Little did I know that it would be three-and-a-half years before my prayers were answered and His promise fulfilled.

I suppose sin was the primary reason that God delayed His promise. I was trying hard to adhere to the teachings of Jesus but old habits die hard. My use of profanity was less but still a part of my vocabulary. My anger was much more under control, and I discovered the less I swore, the less my anger exploded. Swearing seemed to give me permission to become angry. My alcohol consumption was becoming under control, yet there were times I would drink until inebriated. I could work on all of these very apparent sins, but the most consequential sin creating the separation between God and me was one I wouldn't even recognize as a sin for many years.

When asked by the Pharisees: Which is the greatest commandment in the law? Jesus replied: "Love the Lord your God with all your heart and with all your soul and with all your mind." This is the first and greatest commandment. And the second is: "Love your neighbor as yourself." I had closed my heart to loving or accepting love, so it wasn't possible for me to love God. I didn't love myself so I couldn't love my neighbor. I had dared to risk being vulnerable by giving unconditional love to another person only a handful of times in my life. Thus, in retrospect, it's apparent why God withheld His promise of a relationship for over three years. The two most important charges from God are love- centered, but love, for me, was a word, not an experience.

I spent the following three-and-a-half years chasing after God. These years may have been crucial to a lasting walk with Christ, since it was during this time that I was able to build my faith on a solid foundation. I can't say there weren't days of frustration with my lack of progress, but I believed that Christ always keeps His promises, and it was only a matter of time before He revealed Himself to me.

I learned to distinguish the voice of the Holy Spirit from my own thoughts and from the temptations of Satan. God's Spirit gave me new and truthful insights to passages of scripture, and He began to impart to me the beginning of an awareness and discernment that was both eye-opening and exciting.

I was still struggling with my prayer life. My mind would drift off in the middle of a prayer. I would pray thanks for His blessings and pray intercessory prayers, but my feeling of unworthiness trumped any personal pleas. There were times when I would cease a prayer in mid-sentence because I felt no one was listening. The one prayer that I asked unceasingly was to have a true relationship with Him. I continued to ask, seek and knock with a persistence that bordered on nagging, much like the man who knocked on his friend's door at midnight asking to borrow three loaves of bread. I prayed with "boldness."

Once I took this huge leap of faith by committing my life to this unseen God, only then was I determined not to settle. I refused to settle for the Sunday morning worship music, for Pastor Rob's sermons, for the community of our small groups, or for the reading of the Word. I wanted these and more. I was convinced of the truth of the Gospel beyond a shadow of a doubt, and I wasn't searching for further proof. I simply wanted every promise that Christ offered and was willing to bestow on me, beginning with an as yet undefined relationship with Jesus, and I was ready to do my part.

Sin separated us. There was so much for me to work on that, at times, the very volume of my sin overwhelmed me. Anger, alcohol, bitterness, unforgiveness, remoteness, and profanity were just some of the demons that I was battling at the time. I didn't know where to begin until the Holy Spirit took charge. He began to prioritize which sin to confess, repent, and pray about through thoughts He would root in my mind. Some, like profanity, were defeated by sheer will power, while others, like unforgiveness, were both painful and tough to overcome, and would have been impossible to beat without God's intervention.

Whenever a noise, a smell, a name, a song, or any such stimulus would recall a painful memory to mind, I had the ability to send it back to some mental file cabinet, where it would fester until it was summoned once again. Through the prompting of the Spirit, I found I must allow these hurtful memories to linger, and I needed to grieve them, confess, and repent my part as each presented itself. Only then was I free from them. It was a long, arduous, and painful process.

It took years to clean up the junk accumulated from past transgressions, false beliefs, and worldly value systems. Even now, some ten years later, an ugly memory that hasn't been settled will suddenly reemerge and have to be dealt with. Although I have been forgiven for these offenses by the blood of Christ on the cross, it was necessary to endure this grieving process so as to forgive myself and to free myself from the bondage (guilt) of past sins.

I was beginning to understand the true meaning of freedom, a freedom that can only be experienced by walking in the light. I had been a poser and a liar for so long that this newfound freedom was so exhilarating, it sometimes took my breath away. Before Christ, in the morning upon wakening, I would have to rehash the events of the day before to insure that I kept my stories straight so as not to be caught in an untruth or exaggeration. Most of my lies were told to make me seem better than I was, to reinforce the false image I had created of myself, but they were lies nevertheless. After Christ I awoke with a clear conscience and had nothing to hide from anyone. It seemed as God helped me with unforgiveness, my bitterness lessened, and as I worked on my profanity, my anger began to diminish. Great strides were made, but I had a nagging sense that there was another river to cross before I would know God on a deeper, more intimate level.

But all I could do was obey and continue the chase.

CHAPTER 11

DRENCHED

I knew something had to change if I was to be a voice for Christ, because as I matured intellectually, my witness became less and less effective. As strong as I believed my faith to be, my evangelizing sounded hollow, and my empty words echoed back to me with so little conviction that I would feel a flush of shame and embarrassment as I looked into the perplexed eyes of a seeker who would politely nod his head.

In retrospect I've discovered my personality doesn't allow me to speak convincingly without having experienced the topic. I need to feel or touch or have been impacted experientially in some manner in order to convey, effectively, the truth to others. Otherwise I feel like a bad actor who is simply reciting someone else's words of something I know little or nothing of.

This pursuit of God went on for more than three years. I can't say there weren't times when I became frustrated, but never did I lose faith in either Jesus or His promises. When my exasperation was at its height, I was able to remember my life before Christ and glory in the change. If it was God's will to not grant my desire, I, at the very least, had His Son in my life, His spirit in my soul, and His assurance of eternal life with Him. Could anyone desire a greater consolation prize?

Once a year our church hosts a weekend of teaching and workshops stressing prayer and healing and listening for God. We call it the *Holy Spirit Conference* because we invite the Holy Spirit to come among us in powerful ways. It was early on in my walk with Christ when I attended the first *Holy Spirit Conference*, and since I tend to be cynical by nature, I observed the activities with a jaundiced eye. I didn't question the possibility of supernatural events, since scripture is replete with miracles, but I did judge some of the people who received healings and was much too skeptical, and not very Christian, during the entire process. As we'll see, God has a way of making His point.

There seemed to be little or no headway during the ensuing years. In truth God seemed even more distant. But just as I would reach a point of extreme disappointment, I would hear a whisper of encouragement from the Holy Spirit and renew the chase. A few months before the event, the date of this particular year's *Holy Spirit Conference* was announced, and given my reaction to the previous ones, I decided not to attend. Within days of this decision, the Holy Spirit deluged me with messages, delivered in dreams and thoughts, virtually warning me not to miss this year's weekend. It became so intense that I was anticipating the date with all the excitement of a kid eagerly awaiting Christmas. I prepared by keeping my confessions current, quickening my prayer life, and I fasted for the two weeks preceding the weekend. I couldn't wait.

The day finally arrived. We began on Friday evening with worship and the guest teachers setting the theme for the weekend. The sessions were conducted on Friday evening, all day Saturday, and after Sunday service until about 6 pm. These were taught by our pastor, Rob Reimer, Martin Sanders, and Ron Walborn, each of whom were experienced and anointed men who were powerfully used by God. Friday night passed and then Saturday's activities ended without incident. I was overwhelmed by disappointment and frustration, and on the ride home I informed my wife, as a petulant child might, I wouldn't attend Sunday's session.

We went to Sunday service, and once again the Holy Spirit prodded me to remain for the final teaching. I reluctantly obeyed. The Holy Spirit was with us in power on Sunday. There were physical and emotional healings, manifestations, and deliverances, while His presence was palpable in the auditorium, and it was awesome to watch Him work His miracles. And then it was over, and I felt so deflated and embarrassed that I had fooled myself into believing that God wanted me there for some important personal reason. As I began to put on my coat, I heard Pastor Rob call for anyone needing prayer to come down to the front where a prayer team was assembled.

I threw off my coat and actually ran down the aisle to the front of the auditorium, and as I did I had the distinct impression from the Holy Spirit, I was to have Ron Walborn pray over me. (Ron would eventually go on to lead the Alliance Theological Seminary and Nyack College in New York.) Even though I was first in the queue, I had to wait while Ron prayed with a brother and an assistant pastor who were members of the prayer team. As I waited I realized I hadn't any idea what my prayer request should be. After waiting for what seemed to be an eternity, Ron called me to him and asked how he might pray for me. I blurted out that I wouldn't let anyone get close to me nor would I allow myself to love unconditionally because I didn't dare risk being emotionally hurt. These words surely came from the Holy Spirit, for though I was aware of this condition, I didn't consider it a problem, and it would have been the last of my many issues I may have asked to be healed.

Ron put his hand on my chest, and I immediately felt this wall of protection I had erected around my heart being sucked out, as if with a siphon, and being replaced instantaneously with feelings of peace and joy, but even these feelings were overpowered by a blast of love so strong and overwhelming that I began to sob uncontrollably. I knew I was experiencing God's love, and that love took the form of a light so overwhelming, it was as if a thousand spotlights were switched on, illuminating every secret place in my very being. The light was so real and so bright, I was afraid to open my eyes lest it blind me. I continued to sob, but even the tears were a gift from God, for the more I cried, the more I felt a freedom, an unburdening from the pride and inhibitions that had kept me prisoner for so much of my life. I remember thinking, "I'm being touched by God," and this omnipotent, omniscient God, this God who created everything, has allowed me to taste His love. He actually wants me, a serial sinner, who was addicted to violence and alcohol, who turned his back on Him and hated his neighbor, who was an adulterer and rationalized robbery and murder, to be adopted into His family. I realized the person who ran down the aisle five minutes before was not the same man who returned to his seat both elated and humbled. And as the light of God's love slowly dimmed, I was positive nothing would ever be the same.

It wasn't.

But first I need to make something perfectly clear. When I spoke of chasing God for a personal relationship, I was seeking a sense of His presence. No more, no less. I had heard Pastor Rob preach on the *Baptism of the Spirit*, but I hadn't any concept of its meaning. So for anyone who may think that I wanted this experience so badly I conjured it up, I say to you, I don't think it possible to invent an experience I wasn't even aware existed. There will be skeptics, but no one could or will ever convince me that the living God didn't touch me.

Why did God choose me to experience such a rare and life-changing event? I don't know and, frankly, I don't care. I have long since ceased trying to fathom God's mysterious ways. I do know He didn't choose me for my morality or character, and I do know the consequences of His choice. I was immediately obsessed with witnessing about my experience to anyone who would listen and to a great many who wouldn't. Prior to my *"drenching"* I wouldn't speak if there were more than two other people in the room; now I couldn't keep quiet. I volunteered to visit various small groups in our church to give my testimony and witness to the glory of God's love. I spoke before the congregation and the senior class of a local high school and to a college audience. Public speaking was so far out of character for me that my family was shocked. They remembered me hiding under the bed when relatives came to visit so as to avoid talking to them. Later on I began to research the phenomenon of the Baptism of the Spirit and discovered my obsession with witnessing wasn't the exception but the norm. In Acts 1:8 Jesus tells the Apostles, "You will receive the power when the Holy Spirit comes on you; and you will be my witnesses…" Peter's first act after receiving the Spirit was to witness to the crowd that had gathered to investigate the sound of the blowing wind. When reading through Acts, the Baptism of the Spirit is always associated with power, testimony, witness, and service. I was amazed. Here I was acting so far out of my comfort zone that I wasn't in the same zip code, doing things I had never dreamed of attempting, and then reading how God uses the Spirit with exactly the same results on thousands upon thousands of others.

I related how the Spirit had torn down the barriers I had so carefully constructed around my heart over many years. As an example, except for a few tears of frustration, I hadn't allowed myself to cry for over fifty years. I didn't cry when my grandmother or my father passed away, and I had the ability to block out anything with the potential to hurt me emotionally. Now I tear up daily. I have trouble uttering the name of Jesus without getting a lump in my throat and having to choke back the tears. Just saying His name reminds me of His awesome love and invokes the memory of that late Sunday afternoon when I stood in His presence, and for a few too-short minutes, His attention was focused solely on me. I wasted most of the little time we are allotted here on Earth by focusing my energy on protecting me from emotional pain. I wasn't willing to chance being hurt, and therefore I forfeited any chance for happiness.

Earlier I questioned why God chose my hardened heart as the one affliction to heal that day. The answer seems so simple to me now. Jesus said the greatest commandments are to love God with all your heart, soul, and mind and to love your neighbor as you love yourself. The only thing I knew about love was how to avoid it. How could it be possible for God to use me if I refused to bestow or receive love? Since He allowed me to feel His love, I understand the power of love and how it has the potential to heal this flawed and fallen world.

Another of the gifts received with the Baptism of the Spirit is assurance, an assurance of our salvation and the truth of our beliefs. The real importance of this confidence is we are able to convey it to seekers and doubters. We don't need to talk of hope; we can speak of it with certainty. There isn't any doubt; we know the truth.

Suddenly *"born again"* had a new meaning. I was like a child who was experiencing every thought, every sight, and every relationship for the first time. I looked forward to each new day with a feeling of anticipation I hadn't felt since the birth of my children. Every morning was the dawn of an exciting new challenge, new blessing, or new revelation from God, and I began to rise at 3 a.m. to read scripture and meditate in order to "jump-start" the day and experience whatever He may have in store as soon as possible.

And, like a child's first steps, this was only the beginning!

CHAPTER 12

SHELTER FROM THE STORM

Nothing was ever the same. It began on the ride home as I tried to describe the event to my wife, Joan. I couldn't say the words without crying, and I hadn't cried for decades. Finally Joan asked me to wait until we got home, because she was afraid we would have a car accident. I had a near uncontrollable compulsion to witness my Baptism of the Spirit to anyone who would listen and especially to those who wouldn't. I was filled to overflowing with awe and humility and joy and peace and love; especially love. After experiencing God's love being poured out on me, I wanted to share it with everyone I met. At long last love wasn't just a four-letter word; it was real. It was a palpable, living thing that had breadth and length and height and depth and meaning.

There were so many immediate corrections to me as God's creation that, even now, are mind-boggling. My heart was free to feel again, my very soul was at peace for the first time in my life. I was filled with a joy that I had never experienced, I was capable of receiving and giving love, and I knew a humility that was beyond words. Man does not have the words to adequately describe an encounter with God; such adjectives do not exist. Perhaps only speaking in tongues can provide a definitive description.

I began to call myself a new man, until I recognized that I had, once again, become that innocent young boy whom I wrote about in earlier chapters. I wasn't a new man; I was now the person who God meant me to be when he formed me in my mother's womb. I no longer pretended to be someone I wasn't, and how others thought of me (once so very important) now mattered little. Of course I would prefer to be liked, but for the first time in many, many years, I wasn't posing. I was presenting to everyone I met the real me, and if they didn't like who I was, so be it. My desire was to please my God, and I was at peace with Him.

It was a season on the mountaintop, and Godly events began to occur in rapid succession. The following events may not be reported chronologically, because some were unfolding simultaneously while others were drawn out over a span of time.

Marrying Joan became paramount. My divorce from my first wife, Peggy, was in the process of being filed with the courts, but until my drenching of the Spirit, I didn't view marriage as being that vital. I ignored God's plan for a man and a woman (one man, one woman in marriage) and rationalized our relationship with the usual excuses: How can our situation be judged wrong when we love each other? After all, isn't God about love? We are committed to each other, and so we don't need any legal document to bind us together. We don't have to conform simply to please other people. I even used scripture to illustrate that even Christ cautioned against remarriage after divorce: "I tell you that anyone who divorces his wife, except for marital unfaithfulness, and marries another woman commits adultery." Matthew 19:9. Of course, taken in context, Jesus was chiding the Pharisees on divorce, not adultery, but why ruin a good argument with the facts? After my encounter with God, these counterfeit assertions melted away and being married took center stage.

I have always hesitated to tell this side of our story, because I don't wish to encourage anyone to live together without marriage and use our witness to reinforce their lifestyle, but God blessed our marriage. Our relationship seemed brand new, and we found ourselves more in love than ever. We confessed, repented, tried to make it right, and there was no more guilt or shame. Simply put, Jesus redeemed our sin on the cross.

Due to our circumstances I had become distanced from my kids. Although I was welcome to visit any time, Joan wasn't accepted and rightfully so. Joan always encouraged me to see them, but it bothered me to act as if she didn't exist. Peggy didn't want my kids or my grandchildren to know Joan, and I certainly understood her decision, and so, because of my actions, it was hard for everyone involved. You can choose your sin, but you can't choose its consequences.

Sometime during this period Peggy was diagnosed with breast cancer. Immediately, the Holy Spirit convicted me to go to her and pray. Peggy is a no-nonsense, tough, Southie girl, and I thought I knew how she would react if I asked to pray for her. She would look me in the eye and ask if I thought I was a priest, and that would be the end of that. I knew I had to obey the Spirit but I dreaded the moment, and I procrastinated until the day of her lumpectomy. My two kids and I were with Peggy as she was being prepped for the procedure, and the time was ticking down. I still hadn't mustered enough courage to offer prayer, and we had about five minutes before she would be taken into the operating room. It was now or never. With great trepidation I asked the question: may I pray for you? Yes, she replied. WOW! The hard part was over, and now it was the Holy Spirit's responsibility to provide the words.

He did. As I listened for His voice, He began to pray through me for healing and that the surgeon would have the skill to remove the entire growth and that Peggy would have a peaceful calm throughout this entire process. And then He surprised me with a request that Peggy would let go of any anger and bitterness and unforgiveness she may have been harboring. I certainly hadn't planned any such prayer.

The growth tested positive for cancer but the surgeon had removed the entire malignancy and after a series of radiation treatments, she was cancer free.

A few months after her treatments were completed, I received a phone call from Peggy. She said now that Joan and I were married, and Joan was part of the family she wanted to invite us to the family Thanksgiving Day get-together. I was awe-struck. Yet again God had redeemed my sin, and in the process, healed a family. My thoughts raced back to that day in the hospital with Peggy and how the Holy Spirit had taken charge and had been softening Peggy's heart ever since.

Joan and I had committed to Thanksgiving at her brother's house, and so we invited my family to our house on Christmas Day. We exchanged Christmas presents and Peggy gave Joan a photo album with pictures of me as a kid, along with pictures of my children and grandchildren, and then she said something I will always admire her for and will never forget. She said to Joan, "Now that you are part of the family, you can add your own memories to the album." We see each other quite often now and spend most holidays together, all because Peggy and I both heard and obeyed the Holy Spirit. He did the rest.

The following account hasn't nearly as happy an ending. When we owned the package store in South Boston, I became friends with Kevin O'Connor, his wife, Diane, and their children. I became close to their youngest daughter, Rosa, who was born with cystic fibrosis. Kevin would bring her over to the package store most every day, and I would talk to her, give her money to buy whatever she wanted at the variety store next door, and encourage her to live as normal a life as possible, given that terrible disease. I treated her as I would any other kid her age. Our relationship grew over the ensuing years, and I watched her grow into a young lady. Her life expectancy was about sixteen years, but with the constant care she received from her father, Kevin, she seemed to be doing okay.

If you have read this far, you may know that I closed the liquor store, and consequently I lost touch with most of my South Boston friends, including Kevin and Rosa. One night, years later, I received a call from Kevin informing me that Rosa was in a Boston hospital and wasn't expected to survive. Her lungs were ineffective and she had been refused a lung transplant because of other health issues. Rosa asked if I would come into Boston to see her, maybe for the last time. Of course I agreed. I began to pray immediately after ending the telephone call with Kevin, and I sobbed like a baby. I remembered her as a young girl, bubbling with enthusiasm and confidence, looking forward to summer vacation and a full life beyond, and now this.

While driving into Boston on the day of the visit, I thought about what my prayer should look like, but when on the elevator going up to Rosa's floor, the Holy Spirit prompted me to wait and listen. Upon opening the door to her room, I felt the palpable presence of the Spirit. After some awkward greetings I asked Rosa if I could pray for her. I waited for the Spirit for what seemed an eternity, and just as I was about to begin without Him, He took charge. The prayer didn't seem to be anything special, as it touched on healing, peace, the skill of the doctors, etc., and yet Rosa and Kevin were very touched by it. They were impacted not by the prayer's content but by the exchange, the dialogue, the conversational tone of the prayer. They had never heard anyone talk to God as a friend. In the couple of weeks she had remaining, she insisted that she and Kevin talk to God for an hour every night. Rosa had one prayer answered during that short time: she was able to go home to be with her daughter and her own mother for Mother's Day.

Within a day or two after Mother's Day, she was back in the hospital, and soon thereafter she was on life support. Our small group was kept informed and was actively praying for Rosa and her family, and as God would have it, Rosa was to be taken off life support at eight o'clock the evening of our small-group meeting.

Kevin called me with the grievous update that they had just shut off Rosa's life support. I barely informed our group and then I broke down. I cried over the loss of such a special kid, and I cried because she should have had so many more years, but I cried tears of thanksgiving that she was free of the pain she had endured for twenty-some-odd years.

I was blessed to be used by the Holy Spirit and blessed to observe Him at His work. As Pastor Rob says: "God is smart and we are not."

I began to receive words from the Holy Spirit. At first I was reluctant to share them with the person for whom they were intended, in fear of being pretentious or looking foolish, but I always obeyed, and the result almost always accurately addressed a situation the recipient of the word was experiencing. These prophetic words were sometimes corrective in nature, sometimes reassuring, sometimes consoling, but always affirming and honoring.

One of the most difficult words I received was directed to Pastor Rob. I consider Rob a dear friend, and I wouldn't do anything to risk losing that relationship. And so when the Holy Spirit prompted me to inform Rob to guard his motives, I was reluctant to convey the message. I test the validity of the word's source in two ways. First I wait until I receive the word a number of times, usually by way of thoughts and ideas or, less frequently, by a dream or a number of dreams, and then I will test it scripturally. In this instance I was hoping it would prove to be an invalid figment of my own invention, therefore releasing me from the responsibility of presuming to offer my mentor and teacher a corrective word. The Holy Spirit, however, is unceasing. I screwed up my courage, at last, and informed Rob of the Spirit's message, and much to my relief he had been discussing the very subject with his wife, Jen, and received it as a valid word from God. My experience has taught me that the most difficult tasks presented by the Holy Spirit are the ones that have the greatest impact on the recipient and on the messenger.

I have always had positions of leadership thrust upon me; now, for the first time, I sought them out because I hoped it would be a way to pass on the blessings God had given me. Joan and I became small-group leaders, which gave us the opportunity to relate to a diverse group of people whose similarities and differences represented a microcosm of the world in general and the Christian world in particular. The transformation that God performed was never more evident to me than when I began to care for the people in our group with genuine concern. God used our small group to bring a number of people to His Son and to heal a number of broken Christians from emotional problems, wrong thinking, and recurring sin patterns. Joan's mother was a church person her entire life, and when she was living with us, she would attend our small-group meetings. After one very emotional evening, she informed us that she had never witnessed such overt honesty in any setting, especially a Christian gathering.

Jim Anderson and I conducted a drug and alcohol abuse program for people in the church and/or their relatives. Jim, by the way, experienced a very similar "Baptism of the Holy Spirit" at the same *Holy Spirit Weekend* and at virtually the same moment as I. He is one of the most dedicated Christ followers I have had the pleasure to know and love. I became involved in a ministry meant to aid church members as well as local people who, for various reasons, needed help with anything from small repairs, shopping, and transportation to medical appointments, etc. We made contact with the local senior center, where I met a wonderful woman named Doris for whom I arranged rides to her many medical appointments. I drove her myself a lot and came to love and admire her. She was suffering from a great deal of medical issues, not the least of which was cancerous tumors. I would take her to her treatments and pray for her in my car before going into the treatment facility. She was so strong emotionally, but the never-ending appointments and treatments began to wear her down, and there were times when she would cry inconsolably, and it would break my heart. She was getting weaker by the day, and ultimately she was admitted to a nursing home, where she continued to deteriorate. I visited her until one day she didn't recognize me, and knowing as I left that I would never see her again, I felt a sorrow that I hadn't ever allowed myself to feel and it hurt. But if you won't allow in the sorrow, you can't experience the happiness; a lesson that only God could teach me.

I have mentored a teenage boy and am serving my second term on the church's board of directors.

There is more. The social anxiety I suffered with and which has negatively impacted my life has melted away, along with my need to please others. We have our problems, just as everyone else on this broken planet, but we have a certain peace and an unexplainable joy that allows us to know everything will work out for the best in the end. Whenever any doubt creeps in, we simply recall the blessings God has bestowed on us in the past and know He will show up again.

One of the times He showed up was a couple of years ago. I was a collector of Civil War pieces, and one day the Holy Spirit began to prompt me to go to the basement and find a certain grouping of military uniform buttons. I hadn't thought of these items in years, and I completely ignored His advice, but, as always, the Spirit never gives up and His urging became insistent. I finally surrendered. I went to the basement, located the items, and returned upstairs with my hair filled with cobwebs. I then "Googled" military buttons, scanned the items, and sent the scan to the top two dealers listed. Within minutes the two dealers were bidding for the collection. The bidding started at $4,000 and ended when one of the dealers dropped out at $10,500. This Godsend came at a very opportune time, and we were able to catch up on some debts, help some family members who were having some financial problems, and, of course, tithe to the church. This is only one example, albeit dramatic, of how God has blessed Joan and me since we have bowed our stiff necks.

I have chosen the aforementioned occurrences simply to contrast the changes that Christ has wrought in me through His love and sacrifice. There are many, many other examples of how He has changed me from someone who hated himself, hated his neighbor, and hated life itself into a man who now knows how to love and how to accept love.

Jesus said: "come to me, all you who are weary and burdened, and I will give you rest. Take my yoke upon you and learn from me, for I am gentle and humble in heart, and you will find rest for your souls. For my yoke is easy and my burden is light.

I have accepted His offer and am living His promise.

CPSIA information can be obtained at www.ICGtesting.com
Printed in the USA
BVOW01s1748080514

352789BV00003B/5/P

9 781457 526329